Cambridge Elements

Elements in the Philosophy of Martin Heidegger
edited by
Filippo Casati
Lehigh University
Daniel O. Dahlstrom
Boston University

HEIDEGGER ON BEING-IN-THE-WORLD

David R. Cerbone
West Virginia University

Shaftesbury Road, Cambridge CB2 8EA, United Kingdom

One Liberty Plaza, 20th Floor, New York, NY 10006, USA

477 Williamstown Road, Port Melbourne, VIC 3207, Australia

314–321, 3rd Floor, Plot 3, Splendor Forum, Jasola District Centre,
New Delhi – 110025, India

103 Penang Road, #05-06/07, Visioncrest Commercial, Singapore 238467

Cambridge University Press is part of Cambridge University Press & Assessment,
a department of the University of Cambridge.

We share the University's mission to contribute to society through the pursuit of
education, learning and research at the highest international levels of excellence.

www.cambridge.org
Information on this title: www.cambridge.org/9781009630108

DOI: 10.1017/9781009630092

© David R. Cerbone 2026

This publication is in copyright. Subject to statutory exception and
to the provisions of relevant collective licensing agreements, no reproduction
of any part may take place without the written permission of
Cambridge University Press & Assessment.

When citing this work, please include a reference to the DOI 10.1017/9781009630092

First published 2026

A catalogue record for this publication is available from the British Library

A Cataloging-in-Publication data record for this Element is available from the
Library of Congress

ISBN 978-1-009-63013-9 Hardback
ISBN 978-1-009-63010-8 Paperback
ISSN 2976-5668 (online)
ISSN 2976-565X (print)

Cambridge University Press & Assessment has no responsibility for the
persistence or accuracy of URLs for external or third-party internet websites
referred to in this publication and does not guarantee that any content on such
websites is, or will remain, accurate or appropriate.

For EU product safety concerns, contact us at Calle de José Abascal, 56, 1°, 28003
Madrid, Spain, or email eugpsr@cambridge.org

Heidegger on Being-in-the-World

Elements in the Philosophy of Martin Heidegger

DOI: 10.1017/9781009630092
First published online: January 2026

David R. Cerbone
West Virginia University

Author for correspondence: David R. Cerbone, dcerbone@mail.wvu.edu

Abstract: This Element examines a central concept in Heidegger's philosophy – being-in-the-world – one of his most fundamental characterizations of our (Dasein's) way of being. Central is an exegetical and interpretive account of the concept as it figures in Division One of *Being and Time*, as well as an assessment of its significance for reconfiguring our understanding of traditional philosophical problems and positions, most notably skepticism, realism, and idealism. Considerable attention is also paid both to the emergence of this concept in Heidegger's lecture courses in the years leading up to *Being and Time* and to his reflections on it in the immediate aftermath of its publication in both writings and lectures.

Keywords: Heidegger, Being-in-the-world, World, Worldhood, Ontology

© David R. Cerbone 2026

ISBNs: 9781009630139 (HB), 9781009630108 (PB), 9781009630092 (OC)
ISSNs: 2976-5668 (online), 2976-565X (print)

Contents

Method of Citation   1

Introduction   1

1 On the Way to *Being and Time*   5

2 Canonical Formulations   17

3 The Significance of Being-in-the-World   42

4 Beyond *Being and Time*   56

5 Concluding Remarks: Further Beyond *Being and Time*   64

References   67

Method of Citation

All references to Heidegger's writings are to the standard edition of *Being and Time* (*Sein und Zeit*) or to the respective volume of the *Complete Edition* (*Gesamtausgabe*) of his writings. References to *Sein und Zeit* are cited as "SZ" followed by the page number, for example, "SZ: 15"; references to volumes of the *Gesamtausgabe* are cited as "GA" followed by the volume number, colon, and page number, for example, "GA55: 19." Most English translations include the pagination of the German original, making it possible to dispense with citing the translations' pagination. Any exceptions are flagged in footnotes, in which case the German pagination is given followed by a slash and the pagination of the English translation, for example, "GA9: 106/84." A full list of these primary texts can be found at the beginning of the References section.

The following abbreviations are used to refer to works of Heidegger that figure centrally in the discussion:

Abbreviations	Volume	*Works of Heidegger*
BPP	GA58	*Basic Problems of Phenomenology (1919/1920)*
FCM	GA29/30	*The Fundamental Concepts of Metaphysics*
IOP	GA56/57	*The Idea of Philosophy and the Problem of Worldview*
OEG	GA9	*On the Essence of Ground*
OHF	GA63	*Ontology – The Hermeneutics of Facticity*
OWA	GA5	"The Origin of the Work of Art"
SZ	GA2	*Sein und Zeit (Being and Time)*

Introduction

The topic of this Element is *being-in-the-world*, a central concept in the central work of Heidegger's early philosophy: *Being and Time* (hereafter SZ), which was published in 1927.[1] Although Heidegger continued to think and write for nearly fifty more years after the work's appearance (he died in 1976) and although his thinking and style of writing changed dramatically over that time, SZ remained a touchstone throughout. A case can thus be

---

[1] One indication of this centrality is its serving as the title for Dreyfus (1991), a commentary by one of the leading expositors of Heidegger's philosophy.

made that having a good grip on this concept is crucial for understanding any phase of Heidegger's philosophy.[2]

Although Heidegger does not use the exact phrase *being-in-the-world* until the opening pages of Division One of SZ, he alludes to it in his remarks very early on. In § 4, after noting how the sciences involve Dasein's relating to entities other than itself, Heidegger writes:

> But to Dasein, being in a world is something that belongs essentially. Thus Dasein's understanding of being pertains with equal primordiality both to an understanding of something like a 'world', and to the understanding of the being of those entities which become accessible within the world (SZ: 13).[3]

That being in a world "belongs essentially" to Dasein, in effect to beings who exemplify our way of being, indicates the centrality of the concept: Being in a world is not in any way optional or contingent. The phrase "*Sein in einer Welt*" (being in a world) points toward the more canonical *In-der-Welt-sein* that appears later and that forms part of the title for the second chapter of Division One ("Being-in-the-world in General as the Basic State of Dasein"). We will have occasion shortly for considering that longer discussion (the interplay between Heidegger's talk of *a* world and *the* world will receive considerable attention). For now, I want to note how this passage connects the idea of being in a world with another central concept in SZ: Dasein. This term is generally left untranslated, which indicates its standing as a kind of technical term for Heidegger. The term *Dasein* in ordinary German simply means *existence*. That is important for Heidegger, but his more technical use of the term exploits the structural elements of the word: *Da-*, which means *there*, and *-sein*, which means *being*. So Dasein means *there-being*, which points to the idea that Dasein

---

[2] One illustration of this is Heidegger's 1947 essay, "Letter on Humanism" (in GA9), written in response to Sartre (2007), which includes him within the ranks of the then-burgeoning existentialist movement in France (Sartre there identifies Heidegger as a fellow "atheistic existentialist"). In his response to Sartre, Heidegger returns explicitly to the project of SZ and not just as a relic of his youthful thinking, but as articulating ideas with which he still identifies (and which are contrary to what Sartre claims to find there).

[3] While I will be citing primarily from the Macquarrie and Robinson translation of *Being and Time*, I will throughout modify their translations, mostly without comment. I'll note here that I will not follow their convention of translating the all-important *Sein* with *Being* (with a capital "B"). All nouns are capitalized in German; retaining the capitalization just for translating *Sein* carries unwanted connotations, namely that the being of entities is some kind of big Being. Heidegger's insistence on the ontological difference – the difference between being and beings – precludes precisely that kind of construal of the notion of being.

is something for whom its existence is there for it, and for whom *being* is there more generally. To say that they are *there* for Dasein is to say that they are understood in some way. These ideas are evident in the two explicative formulations of Dasein he offers early on:

i. Dasein has an understanding of being
ii. Dasein is a being whose being is an *issue* for it[4]

Although they by no means sound equivalent, it is important not to read these as two separate claims. What I mean here is that (i) and (ii) should not be considered as independent of one another in the sense that something might be characterized by (i) without being characterized by (ii), and vice-versa. As a being with an understanding of being, Dasein – the kind of beings *we* are – can raise and pursue the question of being, which further means that it can question its own being, that is, its own being is, for it, a question.

Very roughly, we can say that Dasein can ask about itself, "Who am I?" and furthermore appreciate the *open-ended* character of that question: As long as I exist, I can continue to raise this question, and what strikes me as even a definitive answer can change over time (moreover, anything resembling a final answer to the question will only be available when I am no longer around to appreciate it, but that is a topic for another occasion). If we think further about this question that we can pose of and to ourselves, we can get a glimmer of how *being-in-the-world* is likewise not separate from (i) and (ii) in the sense that to be a being whose way of being is being-in-the-world is to be a being marked by those first two claims. Consider one thing that I might say about myself by way of trying to answer the "Who am I?" question: *I am a professor*. Understanding myself as a professor is not a matter of affixing a label to myself, or having an identification card in my wallet attesting to my being one. Beyond labels and ID cards, being a professor means having a particular institutional status. Insofar as I understand myself as a professor I understand myself as having that status with respect to an institution – the university where I work – and I understand that status as involving various obligations and responsibilities, such as teaching classes, grading papers, writing articles and books, and attending conferences. I also understand that status as intertwined with other institutional statuses: deans and provosts, for example, but also students, departmental administrators, and so on. Notice that even with

---

[4] See SZ: 12 for early formulations of both claims.

just this much we can see that understanding myself as a professor enlists an understanding of all manner of things: universities, classrooms, students, syllabi, referee requests, and so on. Self-understanding is in this way *worldly*: I cannot understand myself as a professor – I cannot *be* a professor – without a considerably wider range of understanding that locates my existence in a broader setting, that is, a world.

When I was a teenager – long before I became a professor – I went on a fieldtrip to a museum of holography in New York City (a quick Google search suggests that it is still there). A hologram is a special kind of photographic image. What is special about it is revealed when a laser is shined through the image on film, which is projected as a three-dimensional image that appears to be there, but in a ghostly way. One particularly striking thing I remember from the fieldtrip is being told – and shown – how the full three-dimensional image can be projected from even one small piece of the holographic image on film: The parts of the film image somehow manage to encode the whole. It is a good idea to keep in mind this special feature of holograms when reading Heidegger. SZ has a kind of holographic structure in that any particular claim Heidegger enters – any particular piece of the project he lays out – can with the proper illumination project an image of the whole. What we've just seen about Heidegger's two claims pertaining to Dasein and their revealing already the outline of being-in-the-world illustrates this idea. Further illustration will be made when we consider Heidegger's claim that being-in-the-world is a *unitary phenomenon* that can nonetheless be considered from different angles. In each case, the aspect under consideration – if considered properly – should lead us back to the whole phenomenon.

This Element will consider being-in-the-world from a number of different angles. Section 1 takes a genealogical approach that considers examples of Heidegger's attempt to thematize the phenomenon of world on the way to his more canonical formulations in SZ. Section 2 considers that formulation in more detail. I there follow Heidegger's lead in treating the phenomenon aspectually, that is, as having mutually implicating aspects or dimensions rather than independently characterizable parts. In Section 3, I step back – as Heidegger does in the last chapter of Division One – to assess the broader philosophical significance of being-in-the-world by considering its impact on our understanding of skepticism, realism, and idealism. Finally, in Section 4, I look briefly at some of Heidegger's work in the aftermath of SZ where he revisits the idea of being-in-the-world in ways that both correct and expand our understanding of it.

1 On the Way to *Being and Time*

1.1 Heidegger's Early Lectures

The phrase that is central to this Element – *being-in-the-world* – can be found prior to SZ. The phrase figures prominently in his 1924 *Basic Concepts of Aristotelian Philosophy* and close approximations appear in his 1923 *Ontology – The Hermeneutics of Facticity* lectures, where he uses "being 'in' the world" without hyphens, as well as "being-'in'-a-world," "being-'within'-a-world," and "to-be-'in'-the-world." However, the ideas that come to be condensed into this hyphenated expression can be traced back even further, to some of Heidegger's earliest lecture courses starting in 1919. In this section, I want to examine some of Heidegger's explorations in these very early lectures that initially point to – and begin to deploy – the notion of *being-in-the-world*. In accordance with the preliminary status of this early material – and in keeping with the brevity of this Element – this section will contain only a series of sketches to prepare the way for our examination of SZ.[5] But these samplings from lectures ranging from 1919 to 1923 provide important insights that will assist us in understanding his more refined ideas; of interest as well are tentative formulations that did not make the cut, so to speak. Conjecturing as to why will prove useful as well.

1.2 1919: *Es Weltet* (It Worlds)

At the outset of Part Two of his 1919 course, *The Idea of Philosophy and the Problem of Worldview* (IOP),[6] Heidegger promises his students that they will "for the first time … make the leap into the world as such" (GA 56/57: 63). Heidegger's vow follows a series of false starts and dead ends in a quest to characterize what he refers to as a "primordial science." By *primordial*, Heidegger is trying to determine what serves as *originary* in relation to the numerous specialized sciences – natural and otherwise – such as physics, biology, and history. A primordial science "will not be a science of separate object domains, but of what is common to them all, the science

---

[5] See Kisiel (1995) for a comprehensive overview of Heidegger's early lectures.
[6] Despite its containing "world," Heidegger's attitude toward the idea of *worldview* is anything but positive. Worldviews are perspectives or outlooks that reflect a person's broader ideological commitments. Although a worldview in this sense might be understood as reflecting or expressing a person's "philosophy," Heidegger sees the goal of philosophy as getting back behind – or beneath – worldviews in this sense. From the standpoint of philosophy proper, worldviews in the popular sense are decidedly secondary.

not of a particular, but of universal being" (GA56/67: 26).[7] None of the special sciences has the requisite generality to account either for their own possibility or for the possibility of the others.

A great deal of the first part of the lecture course is devoted to explaining why psychology is ill-suited to serve as a primordial science. Although psychology promises a general account of *experience*, as well as of the *subject* who has experiences, Heidegger complains that psychology misconceives the character of what he calls *lived-experience*. Whereas psychology characterizes experience as a kind of *psychic process* that occurs *within* the subject, Heidegger thinks that more careful attention to the character of a subject's lived-experience points away from anything characterizable in terms of inner processes: "When we simply give ourselves over to this experience, we know nothing of a process passing before us, nor of an occurrence" (GA56/57: 65). When we conceive of – and talk about – experience, there is a danger of *objectifying* that experience, treating "it" as a something that occurs in the manner of a process or sequence of events whose relation to anything else is obscure. As Heidegger sees it, the challenge is to describe experience without thereby objectifying it.[8]

Heidegger's lead-up to the leap begins with an interrogation of what presents itself as the barest, most general, and in this way, most primordial form of experience: the experience of "there is," which he considers more expansively as "there is something." The generality of such an interrogative gesture risks emptiness, but Heidegger's point here is that even this bare "there is something" goes beyond the model of internal psychic processes whose connection to anything external has not been clarified. Even in the experience only of "there is something," we can already discern something "non-thingly" about it: "The 'relating to' is not a thing-like part, to which some other thing, the 'something' is attached. The living and the lived of experience are not joined together in the manner of existing objects" (GA56/57: 69–70). Relating to is *comportment toward* something, an active encountering – and making sense – of something. In this way, it is already *beyond* any kind of internal psychic process.

---

[7] Heidegger's formulation here anticipates what he will come to refer to in SZ as "fundamental ontology."

[8] The closing section of the lecture contains an extended discussion of phenomenological method, wherein Heidegger presents his idea of non-objectifying descriptions as a departure from Husserl's notion of phenomenological *reflection*, which Heidegger sees as vulnerable to Paul Natorp's objection that phenomenology "stills the stream" of lived-experience. At the very close of the lecture, Heidegger introduces the idea of "hermeneutical intuition," although he does not develop it much there. For more discussion of these methodological concerns, see Von Hermann (2013), Zahavi (2003), and Westerlund (2020).

To illustrate this, Heidegger pivots to a more concrete example, which both he and the students to whom he is lecturing can enact and attend to without having to look any further than where they already are. The "there is something" can be filled in – given definite content – by considering the *lectern* Heidegger is currently using. What Heidegger wants his students to notice here is the familiarity and immediacy in play in the experience of the lectern. The experience of the lectern is not pieced together from a series of sensory processes that involve the awareness of something *less* than the lectern; he and the students do not *infer* that what they see is a lectern on the basis of something they initially discern or have, such as sensations of colors and shapes. There are, Heidegger contends, no such prior processes: The lectern is seen directly by both him and his students when they enter the room, and in more or less the same way. Both Heidegger and the students see it as the place where the lecturer stands. As the lecturer, Heidegger sees it as the place *for him*, while the students see it as the place in the classroom toward which they are expected to look. When the students enter the classroom, they take in the lectern as playing a particular role in what they are up to – attending a class meeting – and the same is true for Heidegger. They thus do not experience the lectern as an isolated thing that then might be understood as standing in relation to other things that are likewise initially experienced as isolated. The lectern is instead experienced *from out of* and *against* the backdrop of a broader environment: the classroom, the university building that houses the classroom, the university, and so on. The lectern is "given ... from out of an immediate environment" (GA56/57: 72). This environment should be understood as an "environmental milieu" that "does not just consist of things, which are then conceived of as meaning this and this." Instead, "the meaningful [*das Bedeutsame*][9] is primary" and this fullness of meaning is "immediately given to me without any mental detours across thing-oriented apprehension" (GA56/57: 73). Although the example of seeing the lectern involves attending to just one item – the lectern – seeing it *as* a lectern involves grasping its significance in relation to the environment in which it has its place. We can think of that environment both narrowly and widely: narrowly, as the immediate environment of the lecture hall and the university, but more broadly as the public realm within which the university is situated. Hence Heidegger's characterizing the environmental

---

[9] I am here citing Sadler's translation, but it would be more apt to render *Bedeutsame* as *significant* to preserve in English the continuity of Heidegger's thinking on this front (most translations use *significance* and its variants (*signify, significant*, etc.) to translate *Bedeutsamkeit* and its variants.

milieu as involving "lectern, book, blackboard, notebook, fountain pen, caretaker, student fraternity, tram-car, motor-car, etc." (GA56/57: 72). Tram-cars and motor-cars are not typically found in lecture halls, but the environment within which lecture halls are found is not cut off from the broader surroundings of roadways and traffic.

Heidegger's appeal to seeing the lectern culminates with his noting that "living in an environment, it signifies to me everywhere and always, everything has the character of world. It is everywhere the case that '*it worlds*,' which is something different from 'it values'" (GA56/57: 73). Heidegger's use of *weltet* as a verb formed from the German *Welt* is nonstandard, just as it is in English (even though "verbing" has become commonplace, especially in American English). Heidegger's "it worlds" here indicates – and emphasizes – the kind of *signifying* that pervades our lived-experience, the "everywhere and always" wherein the lectern is apprehended. Seeing the lectern as a lectern involves seeing it within that "environmental milieu;" the milieu is prior in that an understanding of it informs the seeing of the lectern, rather than the other way around. That is, we do not first see the lectern, the seats, the walls, and so on, and from all that piece together the idea of a university as composed of such things. While it is no doubt true that the university's facilities include such items, their significance flows from university to item. Seeing the lectern as a something-for-teaching-in-a-classroom is an instance of such worlding. The primacy of "it worlds" is further emphasized by Heidegger's differentiating it from "it values." To conceive of the lectern as something with the value of being used for lecturing invites the kind of model of understanding Heidegger wants to avoid: We first apprehend the thing – the wooden box, the brown rectangular object, or what have you – and then assign to *that* the value of being good for lecturing. Heidegger rejects this model not just because it starts with a collection of initially value-less *objects*, but because it relies on a conception of value-assigning *subjects* who are initially isolated or cut off from the world.

Using *world* as a verb – "*es weltet*" – further underscores a categorical difference between the particulars that populate an environment and the world comprising those particulars. The world is not one more such item, the largest or most general thing, "inside" of which all these particulars can be located. To say that these particulars – and the experience of them – *world* does not mean that they are all located in a common space (even if they happen to be), but instead that they *signify* one another in ways that show their interconnections, their fitting together into – and within – a common way of life. They are connected in the way that the words of a language are connected to one another (in contrast to the words making up other languages). *It worlds* is akin to saying something like *it Englishes* for everything that I say or write, insofar as I am speaking or writing in English. Whenever I speak, I am not doing two different things – saying the particular thing I am saying and speaking English – but that what I am saying is in English is indicated every time I speak. Being-in-English is not a further word or bit of grammar in addition to particular words and grammatical structures, but the holding together of all of that into a whole language set off from other whole languages such as German, French, and Chinese.[10]

1.3 1919/1920: Life and the Threefold Sense of "World"

Not surprisingly, given its proximity to the lecture course just considered, Heidegger's 1919–1920 *Basic Problems of Phenomenology* is guided by many of the same questions and concerns that animated the IOP *lectures*. The guiding question of the lecture is succinctly stated early on: "*How do we wish to establish a strict science in this constantly flooding fullness of life and worlds*" (GA58: 37–38)? Again we see a desire for a new kind of science – an originary, primordial, and now strict or rigorous science – whose target is life as it is most basically or fundamentally experienced. Central to these lectures is the interplay between the pair of concepts he invokes in articulating his basic question, the interplay between *life* and *worlds* (in the plural). Life and worlds for Heidegger are only notionally separable from one another: "All life lives in a world. *Overall, what happens to worlds and to parts of the world happens in the living stream and pull of life*" (GA58: 36).

In these lectures, Heidegger pluralizes *world* in more than one way. First, *world* is categorically plural. He distinguishes among three senses of *world*: the *environing-world*, the *with-world*, and *self-world*. Second, what belongs to these categories – particular worlds – likewise admits of pluralization: There are as many self-worlds, for example, as there are selves (living individuals), but even *world* in the other two senses admits of multiplicity as well. At the same time, we should not think of *world* in these three senses as designating freestanding, independent notions; on the contrary, the three

---

[10] And to call them *whole* does not mean that these languages are *complete*, nor does it mean that they are sealed off from one another. Languages can, after all, be translated into one another. This will be important later for thinking about how different worlds are – and can be – related to one another.

permeate one another.[11] Heidegger characterizes "life in the environing world" as an "unstable circumstantiality" that involves "a peculiar *self-permeating* of the environing world, with-world, and self-world, not out of their mere aggregation." He adds that "the *relations* of the self-*permeating* are absolutely of a nontheoretical, *emotional* kind. I am not the observer and least of all am I the theorizing knower of myself and of my life in the world" (GA58: 39).[12]

Heidegger's talk here of *self-permeation* follows on from an illustrative description of worldly life that moves freely among the three senses of *world*. The passage is worth quoting at length:

> Thus, all kinds of things, which lie in the circle of each one of us, and in the circle that is always going along with life streaming forth: our *environing-world* – landscapes, regions, cities and coasts; our *with-world* – parents, siblings, acquaintances, superiors, teachers, students, officials, strangers, the man there with the crutch, the woman over there with the elegant hat, the little girl here with the doll; our *self-world* – insofar as that directly encounters me in such and such a way and directly imparts upon my life this, my personal rhythm. We live in this environing world, with-world, self-world (generally environing-) world. Our life is our world, which we seldom see, but rather always, if also in a way that is wholly inconspicuous and hidden, "are by it": "captivated," "repelled," "enjoying," "renouncing." "We are always somehow encountering." Our life is the world, in which we live, into which and in each case within which the tendencies of life flow. And our life is only lived *as life* insofar as it lives in a world (GA58: 33–34).

Living in – or having – a self world is not something I do separately from living in a with-world or in an environing-world. In living in – or having – any one of them, I thereby also live or have the others: The *self-world* designates the "personal rhythm" of my life, which I live out in a broader array of *places* and regions (*environing-*) in which I encounter myriad others (*with-world*) likewise navigating these places and regions with their own personal rhythms. In the second chapter of the lecture course – starting at § 9 – Heidegger introduces another image that develops "the peculiar self-permeation" he noted previously: What he here refers to as

---

[11] As he notes in his 1923 OHF lectures: "… the environing world, the world round-about, is always there also as a with-world and self world. These terms do not demarcate regions over against each other, but rather are definite modes of the world's being encountered…" (GA63: 102).

[12] Heidegger later in the lectures talks of "contexts of meaningfulnesses" as "continually permeating one another" in § 24b. As will become clear shortly, in these lectures, *life*, *world*, and *meaning* are mutually sustaining notions.

factical life comprises a "multiplicity of telescoping layers of manifestation." The word translated (appropriately) as *telescoping* is *ineinanderschiebender*, which could be clunkily rendered as *pushing-into-one-another*. The clunky rendering helps us to see that Heidegger is not talking primarily about the optical properties of telescopes that allow us to see things up close that are very far away. Rather, he is playing off of the physical structure found not so much with telescopes proper but with instruments such as an old-fashioned seafarer's spyglass whose differently sized cylindrical segments nest into one another (we might also here think of telescoping antennas of the kind found on older cars and transistor radios). Worlds in Heidegger's three senses are related to one another in this telescoping manner: Each "segment" is another "layer of manifestation," a different way in which the worldliness of life is evident. If we compress the telescoping segments completely, we get a broad sense of a public world, but we can expand the telescoping segments by *narrowing* our gaze to consider the smaller segments: First, we can consider the environing-world at more fine-grained levels. Heidegger's example in his earlier lecture of the way the lectern worlds illustrates this: The environing world from out of which things such as trams and trolleys are encountered can be "expanded" to reveal the academic world of the university, which is nested within that broader environs. The sense of *nesting*[13] here is not physical containment, but a nesting of *senses*: The sense of the academic world borrows from – and depends upon – the sense of the broader environing world. In keeping with Heidegger's appeal to *permeation*, we can appreciate how the kind of sense things make in the academic world are permeated by more broadly applicable senses. Although academia has its own specialized range of activities and paraphernalia, much of what goes on in this world carries over from more general and generic ways of living: chalkboards are for-writing-on just as much outside the halls of a university as they are within them.

The environing-world at both levels of description points toward the with-world, which again admits of finer- and coarser-grained levels of description: for Heidegger's audience, one's instructors and fellow students are integral to life within the university, but all of them are related to other others; these relations vary considerably in terms of the level of personal connection or intimacy. One's family and friends make up a dimension of the with-world, but also more or less anonymous others that contribute to the hustle and bustle of life in any particular community (all those

---

[13] Withy and Askonas (2019) also use the term *nesting* to characterize how worlds are related, although without reference to these specific lectures.

(almost faceless) others on the tram-car, for example). We can think of the self-world as referring to the narrowest segment of this telescoping structure, which refers to the particular rhythms and flows of an individual life: *my* life in contrast to the lives of everyone else. I have a biography that pertains to me exclusively and I correspondingly have a pattern of living that is marked by a particular combination of habits, routines, priorities, interests, aspirations, thoughts, fears, anticipations, recollections, and so on. The surroundings that are familiar to me – where I feel most at home – are not familiar in that way to more than a handful of other people (my wife and children, in my case) and even so, my familiarity is differently inflected even from theirs: My activities within our shared residence, for example, center upon different tasks and in some cases involve items that no one else in the house uses (or even knows how to use). That my familiarity is inflected differently does not relegate my self-world to a realm of Cartesian privacy: What is familiar to me are worldly spaces and places, populated by things that are used and spoken of in ways that are common across individuals. "I live in the vital direction of pull into a world, and I live it out" (GA58: 96). I can try to describe this "pull" – the contours and rhythms of my life – which I might preface by saying, "Welcome to my world." But the "I" does not exclude the "we." "We are standing in *our* factical life, and we speak and understand in the circle of our understandability" (GA58: 98). Heidegger's emphasis here on *our* indicates the way the myriad self-worlds found telescoped within the with- and environing-world are informed by and relate to those broader senses of world: "I live factically always *caught into meaningfulness*, and every meaningfulness has its encirclement of new meaningfulnesses: horizons of occupation, sharing, application, and fate" (GA58: 104–105).

Although I warned against hearing Heidegger's talk of *telescoping* as referring to the optical properties of telescopes, there is something in the image of how telescopes are *used* that is applicable here.[14] If we consider further the nesting cylinders of a telescope – or spyglass – one looks through it from the narrowest or smallest cylinder, the eyepiece. Although what one sees from that vantage-point is crucially affected by the optics found in the larger cylinders, nothing is really apparent without looking (and looking from just there). In Heidegger's taxonomy of worlds in these lectures, the self-world corresponds to what in the spyglass is the eyepiece: The self-world is the locus of *life* in the most fundamental sense. Living

---

[14] It is also important to consider that many segments of the telescope yield a single image or view.

individuals are what populate and animate worlds in the other two senses and worlds in the other two senses are accessed *through* the self-worlds of individuals. Although self-worlds are permeated by the other- and environing-world – just as what I see through the spyglass is determined by the optical properties of the larger cylindrical segments – without selves, worlds would be lifeless. We might here adapt Kant's famous dictum about concepts and intuitions[15] and say: Worlds without selves would be empty, while selves without worlds would be blind.

1.4 1923: A Tale of Two Tables

As the title to his 1923 lecture course – *Ontology – the Hermeneutics of Facticity* – suggests, Heidegger here continues, and develops considerably, ideas that had been in play as far back as 1919. The IOP course ends with an appeal to "hermeneutical intuition" as an alternative to Husserl's conception of phenomenology as essentially *reflective*. And as just seen, *factical life* is central to his BPP lectures. The two notions work hand in hand: "The expression '*hermeneutics*' is used here to indicate the unified manner of the engaging, approaching, arresting, interrogating, and explicating of facticity" (GA63: 9).[16] The approach is hermeneutical insofar as it works *from* factical life (the forehaving) and back *to* it: "The fate of our approach to phenomena and our execution of concrete hermeneutical descriptions of them hangs on the level of the primordiality of the forehaving into which Dasein as such (factical life) has been placed" (GA63: 80).

How do these "hermeneutical descriptions" involve a sense of *world*? In the second part of the lecture course, Heidegger offers what he calls a *formal indication* of the "forehaving" that serves as the starting point for the interpretive development of any hermeneutical descriptions.[17] We can understand *formal* here as *provisional* in the sense that the initial pointing leaves open the *content* of what has been indicated. Formal indications require some kind of "filling in." But even without filling in, formal indications – as indications – point *toward* what is to then be interpreted, but also – and importantly – point *away* from conceptions of factical life that

---

[15] See Kant (1965: 93): "Thoughts without content are empty, intuitions without concepts are blind."
[16] Early on in the lectures, Heidegger offers the following characterization of facticity: "'*Facticity*' is the designation we will use for the character of the being of 'our' 'own' *Dasein*. More precisely, this expression means: *in each case* 'this' Dasein in its being-there *for a while at the particular time*" (GA63: 7). Facticity thus refers to the particularity of each Dasein's life, which nonetheless exemplifies more general structures.
[17] There is an extensive literature on formal indication. See, for example, Dahlstrom (1994), Kisiel (1995), Burch (2013), McManus (2013b), and Westerlund (2020).

amount to *misinterpretations*. Both the positive and negative moments deserve consideration. Here is Heidegger's formal, provisional characterization of the forehaving operative in factical life: "The forehaving in which Dasein (in each case our own Dasein in its being-there for a while at the particular time) stands for this investigation can be expressed in a formal indication: *the being-there of Dasein (factical life) is being in a world*" (GA63: 80). As formal, this indication needs "to be demonstrated in intuition." Doing so involves addressing the following three questions: "What is meant by '*world*'? What does '*in*' a world mean? And what does '*being*' in a world look like?" (GA63: 85).

We can work toward answers to these questions by considering the example Heidegger develops at length. Rather than a lectern in the lecture hall, Heidegger instead considers a table in his home. I said before that Heidegger's formal indication points both *toward* and *away*; his handling of the example of a table incorporates these negative and positive dimensions of his gesture. Heidegger especially wants to exclude two prevalent ways of describing the experience of the table and, by extension, factical life more generally. He refers to both in the lectures as *misunderstandings*, that is, ways of mischaracterizing or outright missing what pertains to factical life. The first such misunderstanding is what he calls the *subject-object schema*: according to this schema, to experience a table is to become aware of one object among others in one's experiential field. The table is experienced as a spatial, material thing possessing various properties: a particular weight, shape, hardness, color, and so on. These properties are experienced *perspectivally* by the perceiving subject: At any given time, I see the table from a particular angle. As I move around the table, I see it from a multiplicity of angles; in each case, the table has a slightly different apparent shape, but the changes can be understood as a function of the table's actual shape and my spatial location (along with facts about my height, the direction of my gaze, and so on). The changing apparent shapes thus form a series; the orderliness of the series conveys to me the stability and persistence of the table as an object with a constant shape. I don't see that constant shape directly, but I can infer it from the way the series of apparent shapes holds together. Similar considerations pertain to my seeing the table as having a constant color, which I likewise don't see directly, but infer from the various ways the color appears from different angles (some of which produce patches of glare on the table, for example, thereby making those bits of the table's surface appear nearly pure white), along with facts about the lighting conditions, and so on.

Seeing the table as one object among others divests from the table any and all of its *practical* value. The second misunderstanding Heidegger wants to avoid is evident here: the prejudice of freedom from standpoints. The idea here is to insist upon the primacy of the most *neutral* characterization of the table. The table is manifest as merely an object – one object among others – that possesses in itself a range of properties. Anything pertaining to its practical value is secondary, something that the perceiving subject *projects* into or onto the table. Considered apart from the perceiving subject's interests and values, it is a particularly shaped arrangement of matter and no more. That is what the table *really* is, while everything else we might want to say about the table is subjective imposition.

The key question here is whether we recognize in these descriptions the way tables are manifest in everyday experience. Heidegger wants us to see just how artificial these schemata are. Notice first that these schemata direct our attention to *a table*, a single something-or-other divorced from any kind of setting or context. But in our everyday experience, we do not experience some table or other – or tables in general – but *this* or *that* table, such as the one found in *this* room in *this* house and used for *these* activities.[18] The table is experienced as part of the room, as having been on that side of the room before, but now closer to the window to take advantage of the sunlight that shines into the room in the afternoon. The table has chairs around it where the different members of the family sit, perhaps for meals but also for various activities such as doing homework, writing letters, and working on an arts-and-crafts project. Different members of the family might have their respective places to sit: The elder brother sits *there*, while the younger brother sits across from him, and the parents sit at each of the narrower ends. The daily traffic through the room involves the table and takes account of its presence: Members of the family walk in and out of the room without bumping into the table, various items are placed onto and taken off the table throughout the day, and so on. At the same time, the table is scarcely noticed, but relied upon without anyone's stopping to pay any particular attention to it (no one usually walks around the table to attend to the changes in its apparent shape unless someone has signed up for a drawing class). The table bears the history of the family who uses it: Various scratches record a child's mischievous moment; the discoloration in one corner indicates the injudicious use of paint thinner; a scorch mark

---

[18] My characterizations here convey the spirit rather than the letter of Heidegger's development of this example.

in the middle testifies to a toppled candle. "That is *the* table – as such it is there in the temporality of everydayness" (GA63: 90).

Heidegger's first question for developing his formal indication is, "What is meant by 'world'?" We can work toward an answer to this question by reflecting on the kind of description of the table Heidegger favors as truer to how such things are experienced in everyday life. That kind of description locates the table within a broader *setting* – the room, the house, and so on – and describes its *role* or *place* in the ongoing lives of the family whose table it is, who are familiar with the table and make use of it as they go about their lives. How the table is experienced – what the table primarily *is* – is as *situated* in the world of that family. World in this sense "shows itself as that *wherefrom*, *out of which*, and *on the basis of which* factical life is lived" (GA63: 86). The key notion for understanding the sense of *world* here, as with his earlier lectures, is *significance* (*Bedeutsamkeit*): "The as-what and how of [the world's] being-encountered lie in what will be designated *significance*" (GA63: 93). We will consider Heidegger's more developed account of significance in SZ shortly. For now, let us just consider how he answers the two other questions he raises to fill out the formal indication of *being in a world*. The second of these three questions is: "What does '*in*' a world mean?" The table is something found in a world, in this case, in the world of a particular family. The sense of "in" is a spatial sense, but that sense is not captured by giving the table's GPS coordinates or the like. To say that the table is *in* that world means that it has a *place* in that world and a *role* within that family's ongoing life. The members of the family are also *in* the world, not just by being located in a particular geographical space (although that is true about them just as much as it is for the table). Rather, the members of the family *live* in that world. The members of the family are in the world in a way that is related to, but importantly different from, the way the table is in the world. The table is significant – and has the significance it has – because of its significance to and for the family. Nothing is significant to or for the table: The table is found in that world, but the table doesn't *live* there. Nothing matters to the table, but the table *does* matter for the people who use it, who care for it or neglect it as the case may be. This asymmetry between the table and the people who use it points toward the beginnings of an answer to the third question: "And what does '*being*' in a world look like?" The table is just there in the world, but those who live in the world are the ones for whom the table has whatever significance it has. Again, the table matters to the people who use it: *Mattering* is the registering of significance, which is why Heidegger says that the "being of the world and that of human life are designated in the same manner with the term 'being-there'" (GA63: 86). More on this in Section 2.

2 Canonical Formulations

2.1 Looking Ahead by Looking Back

In Section 1, we considered three of Heidegger's early lecture courses from 1919 to 1923. Here are some of the key ideas:

i. World as a wherein or from out of which
ii. World as a space or structure of significance or meaningfulness (both translations of *Bedeutsamkeit*)
iii. World as coordinate or correlative with life
iv. World as multidimensional, encompassing self, others, and environment
v. World as both categorically and concretely plural

In his 1924 lectures on Aristotle, Heidegger begins using the hyphenated phrase being-in-the-world with far greater frequency. As before, *life* is a fundamental concept: Only what is alive can be said to *have* a world. This is true for animals as much as for human beings:

> Ζωή is a concept of being; 'life' refers to a mode of being, indeed a mode of being-in-a-world. A living thing is not simply at hand, but is in a world in that it has its world. An animal is not simply moving down the road, pushed along by some mechanism. It is in the world in the sense of having it (GA18: 18).

To say that an animal has a world means that an animal is oriented toward – and responsive to – its environment in ways that reflect its needs and capacities. Primarily, there are things that an animal typically does – and has to do – in order to keep itself alive (and also reproduce, thereby keeping its species alive).[19] What shows up to or for the animal is conditioned by those demands: The animal's environment is carved up, so to speak, in terms of opportunities and obstacles for it and what counts as an opportunity and what counts as an obstacle varies in accordance with the animal's nature. What shows up as something to eat, for example, will be very different for a snake than for a deer; likewise, for what shows up as a *threat*. What counts as *a good place to hide*, a *safe place to sleep*, a *suitable mate*, and so on will all

---
[19] See Hägglund (2019) for a recent account of the animal's normative relationship to its environment.

vary in accordance with the kind of animal we are considering. In this way, we can think of the *world of the snake* and the *world of the deer* as different worlds, even if they are located in more or less the same place.

Although Heidegger here includes animal life within the range of what has a world, in the Aristotle lectures, he marks out human existence as distinctive in terms of the form that *having a world* takes: "The being-in-the-world of the human being is determined in its ground through speaking. The fundamental mode of being in which the human being is in its world is in speaking with it, about it, of it" (GA18: 18).[20] That speaking and language are fundamental here preserves the interplay Heidegger registers in his earlier lectures of self and others: In speaking, I talk *about* the world, and I talk *with* and *to* others.

While the Aristotle lectures underscore the connection between being-in-the-world and life, such that the "basic mode of the being of life" just is "being-in-a-world," in SZ, the category of life is hardly mentioned and when it is, it is relegated to a decidedly secondary position in relation to an ontology of Dasein:

> The ontology of life is accomplished by way of a privative interpretation; it determines what must be the case if there can be anything like mere-aliveness [*Nur-noch-leben*]. Life is not a mere being-present-at-hand, nor is it Dasein. In turn, Dasein is never to be defined ontologically by regarding it as life (in an ontologically indefinite manner) plus something else (SZ: 50).

Whereas the early lectures generally were saturated with talk of life – the flow of life, sympathy with life, lived-experience, the intensification of life – SZ is largely purged of all such talk. What motivates the purge is Heidegger's conception of his project in SZ as a *formal* and *transcendental* project. As a development of a *fundamental ontology*, it is necessary to steer clear of any contingent, empirical dimensions of human existence (human existence is his only available – but not necessarily the only[21] – instance of Dasein). Even though it is true that we are biological beings, what pertains to our biology is in no way essential to – or necessary for – being a being with Dasein's way of being.

---

[20] I'll suggest in Section 2.4 that this discursive dimension helps to secure an idea of *the* world, as opposed to *a* world (or *this* world and *that* world). And as we will see in Section 4.3, Heidegger later contrasts human and animals in relation to *world* in his FCM lectures. There he characterizes the animal as *poor in world*, while human beings are *world-forming*. As with these lectures, the difference is in part articulated in relation to language.

[21] See Martin (2013) for a discussion of the complexities concerning the relation between *Dasein* and *human being*.

2.2 Dasein's Worldly Existence

In the introductory remarks prior to the start of Division One, Heidegger says that being-in-the-world is "a fundamental structure of Dasein" (SZ: 41), adding that this structure is *a priori*. He also refers to it – in the title to the second chapter of Division One – as "the basic state[22] of Dasein." A further point in his opening remarks bears emphasizing: After noting its *a priori* character, Heidegger adds that being-in-the-world "is not pieced together," but rather "is primordially and constantly a whole" (SZ: 41). This is in keeping with his characterizing it as a *unitary phenomenon*. Rather than consisting of separate – and separable – parts that are independent of one another, as a unitary phenomenon, it should be thought of as having non-separable *moments* or *aspects* that can be variously emphasized, albeit without losing sight of the phenomenon as a whole. This exemplifies what I referred to in the Introduction as the *holographic structure* of SZ: While Heidegger, in the course of his investigation, concentrates on one aspect or another of what is designated by his hyphenated expression, the account that emerges always implicates – and so brings into view – the other aspects. Illuminating any one aspect ultimately gives us an impression of the whole.

The exposition of Division One accordingly concentrates serially on different aspects of being-in-the-world, segmented (roughly)[23] as follows:

  i. -in- (Chapter Two)
 ii. -the-world (Chapter Three)
iii. Being- (Chapter Four)
 iv. Being-in- (Chapter Five)

The first chapter gives a preliminary explication of Dasein, which, as indicated earlier, emphasizes the way this account should not be construed as a chapter of – or relying upon – any kind of psychology, anthropology, or biology. Put more positively, Heidegger develops further ideas first mentioned in the opening sections of the work: that Dasein's "'essence' lies in its existence;" that Dasein "has *in each case mineness*" (SZ: 42); and that Dasein has its being "as an issue," and so "comports itself

---

[22] The German here is *Grundverfassung*, which, as Blattner argues (2023: 46–47), is more aptly translated as *basic constitution*. Being-in-the-world is not a *state* in the sense that Dasein can be (sometimes) in that state and (sometimes) not in "it." Being-in-the-world pertains to Dasein everywhere and always.

[23] I here depart slightly from Heidegger's own segmentation in a way that makes the respective emphases more perspicuous.

towards it" (SZ: 44).[24] These ideas are, among other things, preparatory for Heidegger's explication of the sense of "in" in the phrase being-in-the-world: Since Dasein is "never to be taken ontologically as an instance or special case of some genus of entities as things that are present-at-hand" (SZ: 42), the sense of "in" at issue in Dasein's being *in* the world is not a matter of spatial-material containment. Dasein is not in the world in the way that water is *in* a glass or my desk is *in* my study (see SZ: 53–54). Even though it is true that each and every one of us is materially located in that way (e.g. I'm spatially located inside my house as I write this), fixation on that spatial sense of *in* only obscures the phenomenon Heidegger wants to explicate.

Rather than any kind of spatial containment, the sense of "in" is here one of *in*volvement. Heidegger traces the German *in* to *innan*, where the *an* designates being accustomed to something, familiar with it, or looking after it (SZ: 54). Dasein is in the world in the sense of being familiar with it and feeling at home in it. The sense of "in" can be understood here along the lines of the way we say in English that someone is *in business* or *in academia*, which primarily designates a principal locus of that person's activities regardless of where spatially those activities take place (and even if they are often engaged in at particular locations, such as office towers or college campuses). Keeping this sense of "in" at the forefront is crucial for understanding how Heidegger explicates the notions of *world* and *worldhood*.

2.3 A New Typology: Worlds from "A" to "The"

Our examination of Heidegger's early lectures in Section 1 documented how the idea of *world* figures prominently throughout. Moreover, we saw how Heidegger in different courses tries out different ways of talking about, and characterizing different senses of, *world* – world as a verb ("*es weltet*"); a threefold taxonomy of self-world, other-world, and environing-world related through "telescoping layers of manifestation;" and being in a (rather than the) world – before finally settling on the terminology of *being-in-the-world*. In Chapter Three of Division One of SZ, he offers a new taxonomy of the senses of "world" that does not correspond to any of his prior terminological and conceptual ventures. This is not to say that all of what precedes SZ has been abandoned. Far from it: many of his earlier ideas persist, albeit without always being designated with dedicated terms, and it will be helpful at various points to refer back to these earlier discussions.

---

[24] See (2021a) for further discussion of Heidegger's notion of *comportment*.

The taxonomy Heidegger offers in SZ now distinguishes among *four* senses of "world." These four senses can be sorted into two categories: a *categorical* sense, which Dreyfus in his commentary[25] helpfully construes as an *inclusive* sense of world, and an existentiell-*existential* sense, which Dreyfus glosses as designating *involvement*. The pairs in each of these two categories can be further sorted into an *ontical* sense, that is, a sense pertaining to particular entities and their arrangement, and an *ontological* sense, which pertains to the *way of being* of those particulars. Here is how Heidegger himself marks out the different senses:

1. "World" is used as an ontical concept, and signifies the totality of those entities that can be present-at-hand within the world.
2. "World" functions as an ontological term and signifies the being of those entities that we have just mentioned. And indeed "world" can become a term for any realm that encompasses a multiplicity of entities: For instance, when one talks of the "world" of the mathematician, "world" signifies the realm of possible objects of mathematics.
3. "World" can be understood in another ontical sense – not, however, as those entities that Dasein essentially is not and which can be encountered within the world, but rather as that *"wherein"* a factical Dasein as such can be said to "live." "World" has here a pre-ontological existentiell signification. Here again there are different possibilities: "world" may stand for the "public" we-world or one's "own" closest (domestic) environment.
4. Finally, "world" designates the ontological-existential concept of *worldhood*. Worldhood itself may have as its modes whatever structural wholes any special 'world' may have at the time; but it embraces in itself the *a priori* character of worldhood in general. We shall reserve the expression "world" as a term for our third signification. If we should sometimes use it in the first of these senses, we shall mark this with single quotation marks (SZ: 64–65).

We do not need to worry overly about the first two notions of *world*, as they are indicated primarily to be set aside. They are not, we might say, where the action is as far as Heidegger is concerned. Indeed, Heidegger says that he will reserve the term *world* as primarily designating the third of the four senses he delineates. Still, that there are four senses in play indicates a certain unruliness in the notion of *world*, and that is perhaps as it should be. Even without yet entering into Heidegger's ontological project,

---

[25] See Chapter 5 of Dreyfus (1991).

our ordinary uses of "world" are varied and not entirely systematic: We talk about the world of stock-car racing, a particular loved one being the whole world to someone, a trip to a neighboring state (or county, or even just a neighbor) as entering a different world, and so on. Some of these uses are no doubt figurative, but we should not lump all of them into that category. Heidegger's own more systematic regimentation absorbs rather than eliminates this unruliness: His third sense of *world*, the very sense he favors, freely admits of pluralization and is naturally spoken of in the singular with the indefinite article – "*a* world" – rather than the definite. Just why this should be thought of as *unruliness* will become clear as we proceed further: Demarcating worlds and distinguishing them from one another is anything but cut and dry.

In exploring Heidegger's taxonomy more fully, we need to confront a question that has been lurking throughout: How, if at all, are we to understand talk about *the* world in contrast to talk about *a* world (and likewise *worlds* in the plural)? Notice already that this one question actually contains several. For example, we can ask about the singularity of *the world* in relation to the first sense. I take it that there is an issue to be raised there, but that is an issue as to the propriety of talk of a (physical) *universe*, as opposed to, say, a *multiverse*, about which I get the sense some scientists see fit to speculate.[26] *That* sense of unity and singularity is accordingly a *scientific* question, which does not properly arise within the project of SZ. And to ask about unity when it comes to the second and especially the fourth sense is to ask about the unity of a *category*: does what it means for something to be a world admit of a unified account? Whereas in the case of the second category, I don't think we should expect a unified account, as the principles of inclusion will vary in accord with whatever kinds of entities are at issue, Heidegger is (clearly) committed to an affirmative answer to this question in the case of the fourth sense – the worldhood or worldliness of the world – as indicated by his talk in his taxonomy of the "*a priori* character of worldhood in general." That leaves the third category, the very one that Heidegger privileges for using the term *world*. In what sense does *this* sense of world admit of a sense of *the* world?

---

[26] For the past several years, I have heard repeatedly a promo on NPR for *Fresh Air*, which features a snippet of an interview with the physicist Brian Greene. In the snippet, Greene likens "our universe" to one slice of a loaf of bread, whose many slices are all different universes. The whole loaf would be, I suppose, the multiverse, although what makes it a *whole* is not entirely clear to me. Then again, I'm not a physicist.

Rather than try to answer this question directly,[27] let's consider more closely a number of aspects of *world* in the third sense in order to see how a question of unity or singularity might come into view. *World* in the third sense designates "that '*wherein*' a factical Dasein as such can be said to 'live,'" which freely admits of pluralization. Such plurality is readily seen in the ease with which we differentiate among the variety of historical worlds – the world of ancient Egypt; the world of the Romans; the world of the Han Dynasty; and so on – but even more so if we consider Heidegger's appeal to one's own "closest (domestic) environment." In his gloss on Heidegger's four senses, Dreyfus warns against "beginning with *my* world" (Dreyfus 1991: 90), as it risks miring us in a more traditional – and problematic – conception of subjectivity. For now, I want to flout that warning. It will turn out that doing so will only reinforce the point Dreyfus wants to make in issuing it. Domestic environments can be understood as worlds. They typically involve a range of various kinds of *places* – rooms, yards, entryways, and so on – as well as a range of various kinds of *entities* – furnishings, utensils, machines, devices, and so on. Worlds in this sense have various patterns of activities on the part of those who live there: departing for work and returning at the end of the day (unless one works at home); preparing meals; sleeping and rising; leisure time; and so on. Such patterns of activity can also be divided into everyday patterns, as well as exceptional patterns, such as those for holidays and celebrations, as well as periods of crisis and disruption (illness, severe weather, power outages, and, as we've learned in recent years, pandemics).

These patterns are *familiar* to those who live within a particular domestic environment. I know my way around my house, for example, as do my wife and children (and even our dogs). I don't have to invest much – if any – thought in how to get from one part of the house to the other, and I (often) know where things are, and even when I don't, I typically know where to look. Someone visiting my house does not have such knowledge, although for reasons that we will get to, most people visiting my house can make pretty reasonable guesses. Domestic environments are idiosyncratic in various respects, so that we can think of certain forms of knowledge as shared by those who live in that environment that observers and visitors lack. Consider the stock example of cooking in someone else's kitchen. Doing so typically involves far more in the way of opening and closing

---

[27] Indeed, a direct answer may not be forthcoming and may even be beside the point. Keiling (2023) discerns a kind of "dynamic tension" between singular and plural senses of *world*. That sounds right to me.

drawers, cabinets, and cupboards than when cooking at home. In my own kitchen, I know where things are, both in a cognitive sense (I can tell you if you ask me) and in a more embodied, practical sense in that I can reach and rummage for various things without giving it too much thought.

Roughly speaking, it makes sense to talk about *a world* whenever we can delineate a *totality* of practices that are bound together and set apart from other such totalities. My own domestic environment is one such totality; the academic world in which I also travel is another. Talk of worlds in this way resists the sweep of Occam's Razor, as the number of worlds it makes sense to delineate is difficult to reign in. Wherever there is a factical Dasein, it makes sense to talk about that factical Dasein as living in at least *a* world, but most likely multiple insofar as that factical life admits of multiple dimensions or sets of patterns that are bounded off from one another. In explicating the fourth sense of world, Heidegger refers to "whatever structural wholes any special 'worlds' may have at the time" as *modes* of worldhood. We shall return to this shortly.

Worlds can be understood as totalities, but the delineation of such totalities is a complicated matter, as worlds do not divide neatly. Worlds such as my domestic environment are totalities, but they are *open-ended* totalities. In keeping with Heidegger's earlier idea of *telescoping layers of manifestation*, my domestic world corresponds to a narrower telescoping segment that points toward, and is nested within, larger segments that bring others and a broader environment into view. That there are always telescoping layers of manifestation means that my domestic world is *accessible* from without. More generally, a world is *accessible* insofar as it includes routines, patterns, practices, and artifacts that are recognizable from the standpoint of a perspective that lies outside of it. Not everything pertaining to a world's routines, patterns, practices, and artifacts must be immediately recognizable; accessing them can include *learning* what they are, how they work, and so on, as happens when we – the *we* who inhabit *this* world – come across radically unfamiliar customs and practices. Such learning is abundantly evident in the efforts needed to understand the *language* of the world being accessed: translation affords one avenue of access, but there is also the possibility of mastering the language in a way that surpasses translating. A corollary of Dreyfus' rejection of the idea of a "private sphere of experience and meaning" (Dreyfus 1991: 90) is that no world is private in an essential sense. Any world no matter how idiosyncratic and exclusive – a domestic environment with only one inhabitant, say – is nonetheless accessible. Sometimes, this accessibility is assured owing to the nesting of that idiosyncratic world in a common contemporary world shared by its inhabitant and whoever is accessing it. Something like this happens anytime we meet new people or walk into a new home, although it will only be jarring to the extent that the idiosyncrasies are pronounced. But access can also be secured without such contemporaneous nesting, as happens when historians and archaeologists strive to learn more about past worlds that are not nested within any contemporary world (owing to their being no longer up and running *at all*). Even the untrained eye can identify a great deal when it comes to ancient and foreign artifacts: utensils for cooking, weapons for hunting or fighting, dwelling places, various tools, and so on.

So far, we have considered, following Heidegger's remarks about the third sense of *world*, examples that encourage the use of both the indefinite article (*a* world) and the plural (*worlds*). How does world in the sense we have so far explored hang together with a sense of *world* as singular, as, that is, involving the definite article (*the* world) and resisting pluralization? In his commentary, Dreyfus provides a succinct answer: "Such worlds as the business world, the child's world, and the world of mathematics, are 'modes' of the total system of equipment and practices that Heidegger calls *the* world" (Dreyfus 1991: 90). What Dreyfus says here does not quite hew to what Heidegger actually writes about ontical worlds as modes. They are not modes of *the* world, but of *worldhood* or *worldliness* (*Weltlichkeit*): "Worldhood itself may have as its modes whatever structural wholes any special 'worlds' may have at the time." If there is indeed a "total system of equipment and practices," then it too is a world in the third, ontical sense, which means that it too – just like my own domestic environment – can be characterized ontologically in terms of worldhood. This in turn implies that such a total system would itself be a mode of worldhood in just the same way as the business world or the world of the child. Although Heidegger says that worldhood "embraces in itself the *a priori* character of worldhood in general," that would not make it a mode of itself. Dreyfus' identifying more local or regional totalities as modes of a larger totality appears to conflate the ontical with the ontological.

What Dreyfus refers to as a "total system of equipment and practices" might count as *the world* in the third, ontical sense, even while it would be a bit of a fudge to refer to other, "smaller" ontical worlds as modes of it. But should we be at all wary of the idea of a "total system of equipment and practices?" How is the idea of a *totality* – a kind of maximal totality – meant to be spelled out here and in what sense is "it" a *system*? At any given time, there are myriad ontical worlds up and running, so to speak, ranging from any given factical Dasein's own domestic environment to broader, more public worlds. Many of these worlds *are* systematically related via permeation and by involving telescoping layers, but worlds in general do not form an obvious system even if they are accessible from other worlds. Consider as an especially pertinent analogy the variety of human languages: Different languages comprise different systems. Just what to include in such systems is a delicate matter, but for starters, we might consider a vocabulary and a grammar. English is one such system (or perhaps a family of systems, depending on how one counts dialects and the like); German is another, as is Chinese, Japanese, Swahili, Finnish, and so on. What holds for worlds in Heidegger's third sense would appear to hold in this case (hence the pertinence of the analogy): It makes good sense to talk about *languages* in the plural and to use the indefinite article (English is *a* language). Moreover, all of them can be regarded as *modes of language*, in parallel to the way ontical worlds are modes of worldhood. That is, ontologically, the various human languages are on a par as all *being* languages, just as all the many ontical worlds are equally worlds. At the ontical level, however, there is no *total system* – *the* language – of which the many human languages are modes. There are just different languages that are all equally languages. They can be made to be systematically related to one another through *translation*: the different human languages are thus accessible to one another, but this can be true without there being a singular language to which all the many human languages belong. This in turn suggests that the sense of talk about *the* world where "world" is understood in Heidegger's third sense is far from obvious.

Worlds are systematic totalities. If they are to be understood as modes, they are not modes of some greater systematic totality. They are instead modes or instantiations of *systematicity*. Systematicity is not itself a system, just as worldhood is not itself a (or the) world. If we wish, as Heidegger clearly does, to persist in referring to worldhood as a sense of *world* – he does, after all, mark it off as a fourth sense of the term – then it would be best glossed as lacking *any* kind of article, definite or indefinite, just as in English[28] we leave off any kind of article, definite or indefinite, when talking about *language*: English, German, Chinese, and so on

---

[28] This is not the case in German: where we would use simply *language*, the corresponding German would still retain the definite article, *die Sprache*. It has been suggested to me that there is no real question of what for Heidegger counts as *the* world, as the "the" here is simply an artifact of the German language. I'm not persuaded by this deflationary tactic, and for two reasons: first, Heidegger could very well in German have named the phenomenon that interests him *being-in-a-world* (he uses nearly that terminology in his lectures); second, there does seem to be a genuine sense of *the* world that merits explication. When we talk about – and distinguish – the Roman world, the Babylonian world, and so on, we also talk – and think – about all of these worlds as having happened in the world.

are languages (in the plural) and each of them instantiates or is an ontical manifestation of language. It would be a kind of category mistake to ask about the grammar and vocabulary of language, although it might be worthwhile to ask if such things as *having a vocabulary* or *having a grammar* belong essentially to language. Rather than say that various ontical worlds are modes of the world, understood as a kind of all-encompassing total system, it would be less misleading – less inviting of the charge of a category mistake – to think of these various ontical worlds as modes of *world* (no article).

According to the third sense of *world*, then, there are many ontical worlds, all of which exemplify *the* phenomenon of world. That is, the phenomenon of world (no article) can, via the practice of phenomenology, be brought to manifestation by reflecting in the right way on any such world. Doing so would not be a matter of cataloging the details of any particular world,[29] but delineating the structures essential to anything's *being* a world. The key idea here is *significance* (*Bedeutsamkeit*): A world is primarily a structure of significance and primarily for the inhabitants of that world. As I noted at the outset, the unity of Heidegger's account of the structure of significance – that signification has a unitary structure that every ontical world instantiates such that it is a world – means that worldhood is a unified ontological category. This is a nontrivial claim on Heidegger's part, to say the least, but it does not amount to the unity of *the world* in his third sense of *world*; indeed, it almost encourages a *disunity* through the idea of a multiply-instantiated ontological structure.

In the 1924 Aristotle lectures where being-in-the-world figures prominently, Heidegger appeals to a sense of nature as the "already-there" ground for any particular human worlds, rather than another region alongside other particular worlds: "Nature is not a being-region standing alongside this world, but rather is the world itself such as it shows itself in the environing world in a definite way" (GA18: 266). And further: "Nature is the always-already-being-there of the world" (GA18: 266). Nature – the natural world – can be thus understood as *the* site for all the many particular human and historical worlds. Although traces of this idea of *the* world as the natural world (or nature) persist in SZ, the view laid out in his Aristotle lectures cannot be reconciled with much of what Heidegger says in the ensuing years. His references to nature in SZ are far more muted and qualified. He says, for example, that in using equipment,

---

[29] See GA20: 228 for an explicit warning against constructing such inventories as a route to the phenomenon of world.

"'Nature' is discovered along with it by that use – the 'Nature' we find in natural products." Nature is here encountered *within* the world and as something ready-to-hand: "The wood is a forest of timber, the mountain a quarry of rock; the river is water-power, the wind is wind 'in the sails'. As the 'environment' is discovered, the 'Nature' thus discovered is encountered too" (SZ: 70). Furthermore, if we look just slightly beyond SZ, to his 1927 *Basic Problems of Phenomenology*, Heidegger is even more clear there that nature is something discovered *within* the world: "An example of an intraworldly entity is nature" (GA24: 240). World here "devolves" upon nature, but as something foreign to it in the sense that nature can be as it is regardless of its having been uncovered, as "being within the world does not belong to the *being* of nature" (GA24: 240). This is in sharp contrast to Dasein, since "to exist means to be in a world" (GA24: 241). Notice, however, the indefinite article.

Despite Heidegger's movement away from a more naturalistic conception of world – in keeping with his movement away from the category of *life* – SZ retains certain naturalistic elements that provide another avenue for thinking about the unity of the world. These elements appear in his discussion of *world-time* very late in SZ.[30] Heidegger's exceedingly complex ideas on time and temporality are well beyond the scope of this Element. I will restrict myself here to noting that his appeal here to *world-time* allows us to make a sense of a unity – a sense of *the* world – that does not just mean a big world made up of all the smaller or "special" worlds somehow aggregated into a totality. A fundamental feature of world-time is time-reckoning, which has what Heidegger calls "astronomical and calendrical" dimensions. This astronomical and calendrical form of time-reckoning points to elements and dimensions that all worlds have in common: passing from day to night; the accumulation of such days; the marking off of those accumulations into further units; the passing of the seasons; and so on. Moreover, these patterns and markers allow for coordination across different worlds. What we might call *natural world-time* points toward a sense of *the* world as a temporal "wherein" for the myriad historical worlds there are, have been, and will be. But the world in the sense of a temporal "wherein" is not itself a further ontical world of the kind we considered above. "It" is not one more "segment" of the telescoping layers of

---

[30] See Chapter 5 of McMullin (2013) for an account of world-time that develops these ideas considerably. Blattner (2005) and Blattner (2023) also contain extensive discussions of world-time but without much consideration of the naturalizing and unifying factors. Indeed, Blattner's account transposes the plurality of worlds into a temporal mode: Just as there are many *worlds*, so too are there many *world-times*.

manifestation, but something more like the principles in virtue of which telescopes have the structure they have. World-time is marked by a kind of *transcendence*, indeed the same kind of transcendence as Heidegger accords to the world:

> That time 'wherein' entities within-the-world are encountered, we know as "world-time". By reason of the ecstatico-horizonal constitution of the temporality which belongs to it, this has *the same* transcendence as the world itself. With the disclosedness of the world, world-time has been made public, so that temporally concernful being alongside entities *within-the-world* understands these entities circumspectively as encountered 'in time' (SZ: 419).

Note here Heidegger's talk of "the world itself" as what is transcendent. Dasein is always *in* one or more ontical world – always familiar and involved with a meaningful milieu – but Dasein transcends toward the world, which is not one more world in Heidegger's third sense of world. What this means is that Dasein is never *just* in a world in the third sense; its particular world as one world among others, one world among indefinitely many *possible* worlds. (To think – or live out one's life – otherwise is symptomatic of inauthenticity.) This notion of transcendence is retained and developed further in many of his writings and lectures immediately following SZ. These writings will be explored in Section 4.

2.4 Worldhood, Significance, and Publicity

From the very first lectures we considered, from 1919, wherein Heidegger tried out the verb-phrase, "*es weltet*," he repeatedly characterizes the sense of "world" (along with those of "worlding" and "worldhood") that interests him in terms of *meaningfulness* or *significance* (*Bedeutsamkeit*). In Chapter Three of Division One of SZ, Heidegger provides a detailed account of significance and its structure. Many of the important elements in Heidegger's account have been touched upon or mentioned in passing since the start of Section 1, but it is important to see how they all come together in SZ.

Let's start, more or less as Heidegger does, by considering the kinds of things we encounter and make use of in our everyday dealings. Rather than mere material objects of various dimensions and with various properties – what Heidegger refers to here as simply *things* – we encounter what he refers to as *equipment*: pens, paper, laptops, coffee mugs, screwdrivers, backpacks, lawnmowers, and so on. Importantly, Heidegger says that "taken strictly, there 'is' no such thing as *an* equipment" (SZ: 68). This is evident already in the barest characterization of any item of equipment, namely, that it is *something-for-something*: The pen is for writing, the backpack is for holding my stuff for the camping trip, the coffee mug is for holding my coffee, and so on. Considering any one item – or kind – of equipment *leads us toward* other things: other items of equipment (consider the interconnection between hammers and nails, screws and screwdrivers, and so on), but also various ranges of tasks and activities (pounding in nails, drinking coffee, jotting down a note), along with a variety of projects (building something, writing an article, getting away from it all). Holding among this constellation of equipment, tasks, and projects are relations of *reference*: a hammer refers to nails, as well as to hammering, and fastening pieces of wood together, building a house or piece of furniture, and so on. These are relations that Heidegger designates as *with-which*, *in-order-to*, and *toward-which*: a hammer is something with-which one hammers in nails, in-order-to fasten pieces of wood, toward the building of something.

Implicit in all of these relations of reference is, of course, Dasein: what establishes and sustains these constellations of equipment, tasks, purposes, and projects is their being understood and put to use in those ways. Concernful Dasein is the animating principle of these various contexts of equipment: what makes a hammer a hammer lies in its being *used* as a hammer; divorced from – or divested of – that use, the hammer *is* no longer equipment, but only a mere thing. Heidegger makes this animating principle explicit in the final referential relation that holds all the other relations together – *for-the-sake-of* – which refers explicitly to Dasein's self-understanding, what it takes itself to be up to or doing in putting equipment to use in various ways. Heidegger calls the for-the-sake-of the "primary 'towards-which,'" which "pertains to the being of *Dasein*, for which, in its being, that very being is essentially an *issue*" (SZ: 84). All the other referential relations are subordinate to – and dependent upon – this principal relation. Equipment is constituted by its *involvement* in this web of relations – involved in *these* ways and for *these* purposes – and equipment is thereby, as Heidegger puts it, "freed" for this involvement through – and in relation to – Dasein's concernful activity. We can think of this talk of freeing as operative at different levels: When I head downstairs to the kitchen for a cup of coffee, my trusty coffee mug stands out, along with the coffee pot, as most salient for what I am up to; in that way, it is freed for its involvement in my drinking a cup of coffee, in contrast to the many other things that populate my kitchen but mostly lurk in the background as I pour myself a cup. But this kind of episodic freeing does not stand alone. When I walk into the kitchen to get a cup of coffee,

I am not starting from scratch in terms of what might be put to use for my purposes.[31] When I reach for the cup, I am not thereby making it be a coffee cup, as though for the first time; rather, my actions are determined in relation to a *prior* freeing up of meaningful items of equipment that are involved in various activities. Freeing up the cup is not something I do on that occasion except in the sense of its now standing out that it has been so freed.

Coffee cups are involved in the making and consuming of coffee. As such they refer back ultimately to coffee drinkers, those of us who enjoy such beverages. Being a coffee drinker is a *role* that any of us can take up, and in doing so, I understand myself as having that role, as being, among many other things, a coffee drinker. As so assigned, different aspects of my environment stand out as salient in ways that they largely do not for those who do not drink coffee: coffee beans, grinders, mugs, and so on all become relevant in virtue of my occupying that role. Heidegger calls this way of occupying a role *assigning*: I assign myself the role of being a coffee drinker. The idea of assignment – in contrast with involvement – hangs together with the special status of the for-the-sake-of. It is not up to the coffee mug to play the role it does in our everyday lives, but I can decide to give up coffee, either because I've lost the taste for it or my doctor urged me to do so or for some other reason.

Heidegger's analysis of the structure of significance in terms of involvements and assignments leads ultimately to the phenomenon of *world*:

> *That wherein* Dasein understands itself beforehand in the mode of assigning itself is *that for which* it has let entities be encountered beforehand. *The "wherein" of an act of understanding which assigns or refers itself, is that for which one lets entities be encountered in the kind of being that belongs to involvements and this "wherein" is the phenomenon of world* (SZ: 86).

To which he adds: "And the structure of that to which Dasein assigns itself is what makes up the *worldhood* of the world" (SZ: 86).

Another dimension of Heidegger's account of worldhood, while already implicit in what we have considered so far, gets treated more explicitly in Chapter Four of Division One. Recall that Heidegger's earlier typology of world – in the BPP lectures – involved the triad of the self-world, the with-world, and the environing-world. Insofar as we can map that terminology onto Heidegger's later discussion, we can see that the first

---

[31] I am also not starting from scratch with respect to my purposes either. We will come back to this idea shortly.

and third elements of that earlier typology have been treated: Dasein's *self-understanding* is interwoven with an environing world in which various kinds of equipment are involved in tasks and projects that are subservient to that self-understanding. Self-understanding and world-understanding are mutually implicating: Understanding myself as a coffee drinker hangs together with all of the various gear for making and consuming coffee, as well as the skills and techniques for making coffee, not to mention the various kinds of farms, shops, cafes, and other venues implicated in the production, sale, and consumption of coffee. It is important, however, that we not lose sight of the middle element, the with-world; otherwise, as Dreyfus worries in his commentary when it comes to starting with the world of the self, we are liable to understand Dasein as a kind of meaning-giving *subject*, who projects or imposes individually meanings onto what are otherwise bare objects. That this is not so is already evident in the way I described my trip to the kitchen to get a cup of coffee. While my doing so just then is a result of my having decided to get another cup of coffee, I do not in that episode – or really at any time beforehand – *decide* what is to *count as* a coffee cup (or coffee, a coffee maker, a kitchen, and so on). While there might be times – on a camping trip, say – where I'll have to poke around and find something that will suffice as a makeshift coffee cup, my doing so is still guided by a prior understanding of what coffee cups are. That prior understanding is something I *acquired* from growing up in surroundings already populated by things like coffee cups and coffee makers. What coffee cups are, how they are to be properly used (as opposed to all the things they *can* be used for, like holding pencils or drinking orange juice), and so on are things I learned – or discovered – about my world rather than anything I devised or decided.

If we then ask *who exactly* decided these things, it is not entirely clear at whom we might point. Of course, for particular kinds of things – Velcro, for example, or Post-It notes – there might be a particular person or group of people we can single out as being responsible for there being such things and for having at least some authority on how they are to be used (although that authority is limited, as once the inventions begin to circulate, how they are to be used can change dramatically). There are, however, limits to this kind of pointing out, since those particular inventions were devised and created in an already-given context replete with lots of already-meaningful items with designated proprieties of use. That kind of inventing or devising cannot, so to speak, go all the way down. Similar considerations pertain to the meanings of words. While sometimes a particular person or group of people is responsible for coining a new word, we cannot apply the model of coinage to language as a whole. How would the "first" words be introduced? How would their meaning be explained? And as already noted with inventions, coined words will often change meanings or take on new ones irrespective of the intentions of the original coiner.

What we find in everyday life is a kind of *authority* – *this* is called (and used as) a coffee cup; *this* is called (and used as) a pencil; and so on – but without any specifiable *authority figure*. Heidegger calls this anonymous authority *das Man*, sometimes translated (unhelpfully) as *the "they*," but more accurately translated as "the one" (although that can be misleading, as it suggests a kind of solitary and all-powerful authority figure). Translators have often instead reached for *the Anyone* to convey the way this kind of authority holds sway within a shared, communal world. Everyone experiences this authority as binding on them in more or less the same way, as *das Man* "articulates the referential context of significance" (SZ: 129), in other words, the everyday world. Indeed, the authority is so pervasive that we largely don't notice it at all, except in cases where there are deviations from how things are usually done or from what things are usually called (as when we see someone stirring paint in a coffee cup or using a hammer to prop open a window).

Even when I'm alone, this kind of anonymous authority is still operative in that I recognize and make use of things in largely generic ways: I drink coffee from a mug as any*one* does, toast bread as any*one* does, think to myself – and talk to the dogs – in English as any*one* does, and so on. Although there may be quirks or idiosyncrasies in how I do things, especially when I am by myself, what's quirky or idiosyncratic about such things will still be readily recognizable to, and understandable by, others. And, of course, I am (happily) not always alone. The worlds we by and large navigate are not just pervaded by an anonymous authority that refers to everyone and anyone, but they are populated by *others*. This is something Heidegger emphasizes from the start: His *es weltet* encompasses not just various bits of equipment and distinctive locales, but various people, some of whom play particular roles (he mentions a caretaker, for example). In the *BPP* lectures, where the idea of a with-world is introduced, Heidegger discusses the communal dimension at length, noting how "*every human being carries within himself a reserve of intelligibilities and immediate accessibility*" (GA58: 34). What these reserves contain vary across times and cultures – and sometimes in various ways even across town! – but the important thing is that they are shared. We also saw earlier in this section how Heidegger emphasizes speech and language in the Aristotle lectures: Speaking is generally a speaking-with and speaking-to using a language that is by and large shared.

What Heidegger earlier called the with-world is absorbed into an aspect of Dasein's way of being. He calls this aspect of Dasein's constitution *being-with*. One important dimension of this designation is that it signals a fundamental difference in the way Dasein understands others as compared with items of equipment. Heidegger refers to our ways of engaging with equipment forms of *concern*, ways of taking up and taking care of things, although we have to remember that being neglectful, careless, and irresponsible are modes of concern (the latter are what Heidegger refers to as *deficient* modes of concern). His name for our ways of engaging with one another he refers to instead as *solicitude*. Greeting one another is one form solicitude takes, but so is snubbing, ignoring, and offending. Even if someone's attitude toward others is largely strategic and manipulative, what is involved in manipulating another person – and what forms of censure that might elicit – is fundamentally different from the forms manipulating equipment might take.

2.5 Aspects of Being-In

As we saw in Section 2.2, Heidegger begins his explication of being-in-the-world by emphasizing the distinctive sense of "in" at work in the expression so as to ward off the idea that it primarily denotes spatial containment. The "in" instead denotes *involvement* and *familiarity*: Insofar as Dasein *is*, it has a world (or worlds) with which it is familiar. In Chapter Five of Division One, Heidegger circles back to this distinctive sense of "in," this time in tandem with the preceding "being," to investigate in greater detail the structural dimensions of Dasein's familiarity with the world. In the chapter, Heidegger covers a great deal of ground. Among the topics are *moods, thrownness, understanding, interpretation, assertion, language, idle talk, curiosity, ambiguity,* and *falling*. Rather than try to take all of this on, I will focus on the three most fundamental aspects of being-in – *Befindlichkeit* (why I leave it untranslated will be explained); *understanding*; and *discourse* – plus one more – *falling* – whose status is less clear. Not only are these the most fundamental aspects of Heidegger's account in this chapter, they also connect most readily with what we have examined so far.

Let's start, as Heidegger does, with *Befindlichkeit*. The term poses extra challenges for translation, as it is Heidegger's coinage, and so what meaning it has lies in what he does with it in his account. The term does incorporate standard German, however, as it plays off of an everyday question (indeed, it is one of the first questions one learns in an elementary German class): "*Wie befinden Sie sich?*" which is most naturally translated as, "How are you doing?" Heidegger, however, is drawing on the *finden* bit of the question, as his term emphasizes a sense of our *finding ourselves* as already situated and disposed in a particular way. Macquarrie and Robinson translate the term as *state-of-mind*, which conveys some of what Heidegger is after, but also sounds overly mentalistic. Other translations have been hazarded: predisposedness; so-found-ness; even where-you're-at-ness. Predisposedness is perhaps the most felicitous, as it conveys a sense of one's orientation toward things as being already shaped in some way or other. Very roughly, we can think of this predisposedness as having both proximal and distal aspects to it. Proximally, predisposedness is evidenced by *moods* (the German here is *Stimmungen*, which can also be translated as *attunements*). We always find ourselves in some mood or another, and what mood we find ourselves to be in is not a matter of our choosing or deciding. Some mornings, I wake up eager to get going with whatever it is I'm up to that day; other mornings, all I can manage is just to get out of bed. In neither case did I *choose* to be in the one mood or the other. I might, on reflection, be able to *explain* why my mood is as it is: perhaps I got a good night's sleep on the morning I woke up ready to roll; perhaps I'm reluctant to get out of bed because none of what I have to do that day is especially appealing. Formulating such explanations can sometimes alter our moods and we can often do things deliberately to affect our moods (I know, for example, that on mornings when I wake up despondent that a walk with the dogs will generally cheer me up). That Dasein is always in a mood calls attention to the way our ways of being oriented toward the world are affectively conditioned. We are never not in a mood, although some moods are more dramatic and noticeable than others. Although moods are often understood as purely subjective states, they are world-oriented and world-revealing: Things show up as mattering in various – and different – ways depending on my mood, and a particular mood may just as easily draw my attention to a genuine and important feature of the world (an exciting opportunity, for example) as it may block my view. That we are always in moods emphasizes how, for Heidegger, we are not primarily detached observers (although a mood of cool detachment is possible); rather, the world *matters* to us in various ways and this is registered and modulated by our moods.

I said before that there is a more distal sense of *Befindlichkeit* or predisposedness. This other sense was already operative in the deliberately pedestrian example I used above of my heading to the kitchen to get a cup of coffee. There, I noted that when I go into the kitchen, I do not there and then *decide* anything in terms of what things count as coffee cups (or kitchens, for that matter), and at no point in the past did I make any decisions along those lines, either in terms of what things that surround me *count as* coffee cups or, since I grew up in an English-speaking environment, that they are called "coffee cups." Pedestrian as they are, coffee cups and the label or term "coffee cups" are part of the everyday world that I experience as "always already" having been there. Coffee cups and "coffee cups" are, so to speak, part of my inheritance of a world that was carved up and sorted before I came along. No one ever asked me what to call the things that hold coffee and I only could have been asked had I already mastered a *language* that both I and the inquirer understood. Learning one's first language – which one does in conjunction with learning one's way around a particular environment in tandem with grownups who already speak that language and navigate that environment – is not a matter of making choices or decisions, as those would require already having a way of understanding of the kind that having a language facilitates.

Both the proximal and varying moods that I find myself in from day to day and the more distal ways in which my sensibilities have been pre-delineated and shaped prior to any kind of conscious decisions (as such pre-delineating and shaping are needed in order to formulate and execute decisions in the first place) point to what Heidegger calls *thrownness*. The term is meant to express our having been *cast into* a world whose contours and categories have already been largely determined; moreover, thrownness conveys how we find not just the world but *ourselves* already shaped by the time we are aware of ourselves at all. That is, none of us chooses who we are from the ground up, so to speak. We did not choose our bodily makeup or particular bodily features – having *this* body rather than *that* one – nor did we choose our temperament, basic dispositions, aptitudes, and proclivities. As we grow more self-aware, we can come to understand that we have a particular temperament, and we can get a sense of what our aptitudes and proclivities are; we can even, sometimes with great effort, *change* some of those things about ourselves. In no case, however, can we go back and make everything different from the get-go.[32] Heidegger

---

[32] Later, in Division Two, Heidegger characterizes Dasein as charged with the task of taking over "being-a-basis," while also recognizing that it "can *never* get that basis into its power." Being-a-basis "means *never* to have power over one's ownmost being from the ground up." Both quotes from SZ: 284. The details of how this "taking over" works to modify or modulate Dasein's thrown existence so as to exist *authentically* are beyond the scope of this Element.

emphasizes that there is no getting back behind one's thrownness, which is why I can both sense that had I been born into, say, a family in China, I would be a completely different person, while also recognizing that such thoughts are entirely a matter of idle speculation. Even if I now, at this point in my life, immerse myself in Chinese culture and never speak so much as a word of English again, I will still never be who I would have been had I grown up in China in a Chinese family from the start. Thrownness captures the unsettling thought that *who I am* is purely contingent, but also irrevocable.

Not surprisingly, Heidegger says that *Befindlichkeit* "always has its understanding, even if it merely keeps it suppressed" (SZ: 142–143). I say this is unsurprising for two reasons: First, in delineating these different aspects of being-in, we should fully expect the characterization of any one aspect to end up invoking the others. If we reflect further on what Heidegger means by *Befindlichkeit*, that we are always affectively oriented toward things in a particular way, both locally in terms of mood and distally in terms of a more fundamental thrownness, that this is an orientation *toward things* already suggests some way of understanding what we are thereby oriented toward. If I am in a fearful mood, for instance, things show up to me as threatening in various ways and I show up to myself as especially vulnerable or fragile, but this means that various things and I myself are showing up and so understood as being what they are: I can only be affectively stirred by the sound of distant thunder or a rustling in the leaves if I hear those things and understand them *as* the sound of distant thunder or rustling leaves. Second, that *understanding* is a fundamental aspect of Dasein's being-in-the-world has been evident from the very beginning of SZ, before Heidegger even mentions his hyphenated formulation: What is distinctive about Dasein is that it has a pre-ontological *understanding of being*. This is echoed in the current chapter when Heidegger offers the following characterization of how he understands *understanding*:

> When we are talking ontically we sometimes use the expression 'understanding something' with the signification of 'being able to manage something', 'being a match for it', 'being competent to do something'. In understanding, as an *existentiale*, that which we have competence over is not a "what" but being as existing (SZ: 143).

Dasein always displays some kind of competence over *existing*. This does not mean, however, that each of us always has a worked-out philosophical understanding of either our own way of being or the being of other kinds of things. As *pre-ontological*, we are sensitive to, and register things, *as* being this or that, and, further, as belonging to different categories. Even though no one prior to reading Heidegger has the vocabulary of the *ready-to-hand* and the *present-at-hand*, we all *get it* that things such as hammers and screwdrivers are made to our measure, as reflected in our talk about them as designed and manufactured, whereas other kinds of things, such as asteroids and marsupials, more readily invite the idea of *discovery*. This is not to say that we have a worked-out theory of how to divide the world into the made and the found – and worked-out theories of such matters might vary considerably – but if someone begins talking about the invention of marsupials, such talk is going to require a lot more explaining than what is needed when it comes to the invention of the steam engine.

Heidegger's interest here though is primarily Dasein's having an understanding of its own being: Dasein always has a sense of what it's up to, which is governed by variously broader forms of self-understanding. For example, when my alarm goes off on a Tuesday morning in October, my ensuing activity reflects my understanding that I need to get ready to leave for a full day of teaching. I understand some things as needing-to-be-done because it is a Tuesday (and not a day where I work at home): I need to get the dogs out early, pack a lunch, eat breakfast by a certain time, shower and dress in clothes that are appropriate for a college-level teacher, and so on. I am managing all these small routines and tasks in ways that reflect not just my understanding of what I have to do that day, but why it is that I have to do what I am doing on that day; that is, I understand that I am a professor, that I have a roster of courses that are my responsibility to teach, that I have a schedule for my classes to which I try to adhere (especially if I care about being a responsible professor), and so on. That things appear to me as to-be-done indicates that I am oriented not just toward what is present to me – what I find arrayed in my room when I wake up, for example – but toward *possibilities*. When I get up on a Tuesday, being in the classroom on campus is not yet an actuality. I don't then just sit idly and wait to see if it becomes actual. Rather, it is *my* possibility, which means that it is incumbent upon me to *make it happen* that I be in my appointed classroom on campus at the correct time; in understanding that it is incumbent upon me, I also understand that other things that are, strictly speaking, possible are nonetheless ruled out. I *could* just go back to sleep or pack my camera bag and set out with the dogs on a three-hour adventure or start a day-long cooking project or what have you. These are all possibilities, but mostly they do not even occur to me because I am so bent on getting ready for work. Indeed, that they do not occur is one indication of my general competence when it comes to being a professor.[33]

Heidegger refers to Dasein's relation to possibilities as one of *projection*. When I get up on that Tuesday morning, I project the possibility of being in the appropriate classroom by 9:30 AM – my being in the classroom in a couple of hours *lies ahead* of me – and my projecting *that* possibility is subservient to my more generally projecting the possibility of teaching that course, which in turn … all the way to my projecting the possibility – projecting *into* – being a professor. While I am here and now a professor – whereas on that Tuesday morning when I first wake up, I am not then and there in the classroom – my being a professor is something that I nonetheless have to *sustain* precisely by continuing to project into all the myriad possibilities that make up academic life.

Heidegger says that *"discourse is existentially equiprimordial with Befindlichkeit and understanding"* (SZ: 161). As such, its placement in Chapter Five of Division One appears somewhat belated. Prior to attending to discourse, Heidegger develops his account of understanding to encompass the idea of *interpretation*, which in various ways makes explicit, and so develops, what is already understood. The account of interpretation is then followed by a discussion of *assertion*, a linguistic act that expresses what is interpretively apprehended. Assertions have a predicative structure; they are a matter of saying something of something (Heidegger's example is, "The picture on the wall is askew"), whereas understanding can be pre-predicative. One essential aspect of assertions is their being *communicative*: We make assertions to bring to others' attention various aspects of the world, such as the crooked picture. So by the time Heidegger gets around to discourse, he has already introduced aspects of Dasein's being-in that quite clearly involve linguistic elements. An account of language very much seems called for: "The fact that language *now* becomes our theme *for the first time* will indicate that this phenomenon has its roots in the existential constitution of Dasein's disclosedness" (SZ: 160).

The "roots" Heidegger refers to is what he means by *discourse*: "*The existential-ontological foundation of language is discourse [Rede]*" (SZ: 160). What Heidegger means by *roots* and *foundation* admits of interpretations

---

[33] That possibilities for which we are responsible can come to feel like necessities later becomes an aspect of Sartre's discussion of *bad faith*. See especially his example of the café waiter in Sartre (1998: 59–60).

that differ in significant ways. One way of hearing what Heidegger is claiming here is to see him as pointing to something *pre-linguistic* that serves as the basis for language, for what is properly linguistic. Understood this way, Heidegger is here calling attention to the way Dasein's world is a structure of significance, a *referential totality* wherein items of equipment, tasks, and projects are interwoven with one another. What makes up the workshop, for example, are items with salient differences among them that someone who is at home in the workshop is familiar with and adept at navigating. While I might note that an array of tools all look different from one another, sometimes those differences are slight despite the important differences in their use: pruning clippers, tin snips, and wire cutters don't look all that different, but they should not be mixed and matched. Sensitivity to these differences – and being adept at navigating them – is not primarily a function of knowing the *names* of all these tools, but that they are relevant differences attracts, we might say, different names. As Heidegger notes, "the totality-of-significations is *put into words*" and to "significations words accrue" (SZ: 161). He immediately cautions, however, that "word things do not get supplied with significations" (SZ: 161). What I take this last remark to indicate is that our grasp of language is not a matter of first having an uninterpreted set of symbols to which we then assign meanings. We learn language by learning words and phrases in tandem with learning how to use the things they name. Still, Heidegger's talk here of *accrual* suggests that significations run deeper than meaningful words and there certainly seems to be something right about this. Not every salient difference is marked with a word or words to register that difference and even where there is, I can be sensitive to that difference even without knowing those words (consider our sensitivity to variations in shades of color without having a special name for each variation). I can *tell* that two tools are different and I can even be adept at using them in ways that register those differences without having names for the tools. This kind of telling is in this way prior to telling in the verbal sense of relaying something to someone by speaking.[34] We can see the same pattern of inflections if we consider another favored term: *articulation*. We can think of articulation as a structural concept – something has an articulated structure when it consists of variously individuated parts or segments (think of a skeleton) – but in another sense, articulation refers to speaking. When Heidegger says, "The intelligibility of something has always been articulated, even before there is an appropriative interpretation of it. Discourse

---

[34] See Haugeland (2013: 35–36).

is the articulation of intelligibility" (SZ: 161), that prior structural articulation seems to be what is indicated.

However, *Rede* can just mean *speech* or *talk*, which indicates something *already* linguistic. Insofar as there is a distinction to be marked, it is not one between the pre-linguistic and the linguistic, but rather the *ontological* and *ontical* levels of language. We've seen this difference already, in our discussion in Section 2.3 of language and languages as illustrative of the difference between worldhood and world. In marking out these two levels, Heidegger is not primarily indicating a kind of pre-linguistic phenomenon so much as noting that there is nothing essential about any particular language. Dasein does not essentially speak any particular language, but speaking-a-language,[35] we might say, belongs to its constitutive structure. There is, on this reading of Heidegger's talk of roots and foundations, no point in speculating on whether there could be Dasein without a language, a being with Dasein's form of understanding that never reached the interpretive level marked out by words and phrases, including assertions. That Heidegger emphasizes the intimacy of the relations among understanding, interpretation, and assertion prior to discussing discourse seems to me to tell against such an idea.[36]

We have now considered the three aspects of being-in that Heidegger covers in Part A of Chapter Five of Division One. Part B attends to how being-in is expressed specifically in Dasein's everyday way of being-in-the-world. I will note here only one aspect of that discussion, which calls attention to an aspect of everyday existence that perhaps belongs with those aspects discussed in the first part. I mean here Heidegger's notion of *falling*. Heidegger's discussion of falling seems to call attention to a constitutive structural feature of Dasein, although that constitutive idea is obscured by Heidegger's rather condemnatory tone. (This intermingling of the constitutive and the condemnatory plagues Heidegger's prior discussion of *das Man*.) Most neutrally, falling refers to Dasein's absorption in its present activity: Dasein is always up to something and within the "flow" of what it is up to, there is a present dimension in tandem with a dimension that points toward the past (*Befindlichkeit*) and ahead toward the future (understanding). That falling in this sense features alongside these other two aspects is signaled by Heidegger's summary of the ground he has covered in Division One in the final chapter by means of the *care-structure*.

---

[35] I am using *speaking* here broadly: one can have as one's language American Sign Language.
[36] See § 9 of Guignon (1983) for an extensive discussion of constitutive versus instrumentalist views of language in Heidegger. See, however, Carman (2003: 222–232) for criticism of Guignon's position.

Dasein's way of being – as being-in-the-world – is at the same time *care*. (We have been primed for this by the earlier lectures, with their emphasis on *mattering*, but also throughout Division One. The German for *care* is *Sorge*, which gibes with his earlier talk of the kind of *concern* (*Besorge*) we have for our tasks and projects and the *solicitude* (*Fürsorge*) we show toward others.) In summarizing the care-structure, Heidegger says that "the being of Dasein means ahead-of-itself-being-already-in-(the world) as being-alongside (entities encountered within-the-world). This being fills in the signification of care" ((SZ): 192). The three designated aspects would appear to correspond to understanding, followed by *Befindlichkeit*, and then falling. Notice that *discourse* does not appear here, but instead would pertain to the whole of it.

Heidegger complicates this neutral characterization of falling by citing it as a principal culprit in Dasein's *inauthenticity*: By becoming absorbed in and by everyday life, Dasein *falls away* from the issue of its own existence.[37] Everyday Dasein is "busy being busy" and this absorption in its day-to-day tasks and projects obscures a broader concern for the shape and character of its existence. Heidegger even characterizes everyday Dasein as *fleeing* from the issue of its own existence, which gives to falling an even more pernicious character. Untangling these different senses of falling is important for understanding the distinction between inauthenticity and authenticity. Rather than address that topic, which requires an Element of its own, we will turn instead to some of the philosophical implications of Heidegger's concept of being-in-the-world.

3 The Significance of Being-in-the-World

3.1 Against Epistemology

In the preliminary considerations – § 6 specifically – of SZ, Heidegger characterizes one of his tasks as "destroying the history of ontology." This kind of critical-destructive stance with respect to traditional philosophy is hardly new to SZ, as presentiments of the ideas expressed there in considerable detail are already in evidence as far back as the 1919 lectures discussed in Section 1.2. § 16 of those lectures is entitled, "The Epistemological Question of the Reality of the External World. Standpoints of Critical Realism and Idealism." In § 16 and subsequent sections, Heidegger neither tries to answer the question he names, nor does he align himself with

---

[37] See Chapter 13 of Dreyfus (1991) and McMullin (2013: 109–115) for further discussion of the ambiguities, complexities, and perhaps confusions of Heidegger's notion of *falling*.

either of the two "critical positions." Heidegger's criticisms of traditional philosophical problems goes far beyond offering novel answers to enduring questions or reconfiguring old -*isms* in enlightening ways. Rather, in keeping with the destructive ambitions Heidegger harbors, the net effect of Heidegger's phenomenological practice is to change our orientation toward such problems and positions, such that they are not so much problems in need of solutions or rival positions in need of adjudication as they are the distorted and misguided products of more fundamental philosophical confusions (the framing of epistemological problems is rarely ontologically neutral).

The bearing of Heidegger's philosophy on such traditional problematics – especially his attempts to subvert epistemology – will be the focus of this section. Central to our discussion will be (of course) his notion of *being-in-the-world*. Before turning to SZ and more proximate lecture material, let us consider first his treatment of the question of the external world, along with realism and idealism, in the early IOP lectures, as his treatment there lays down a pattern that will persist into his later writing and lecturing even as some of the details vary. He begins by reciting the cluster of questions that make up the problem of the external world:

> Does my environing world really exist? Is it so obvious that the external world is real and not rather only my representation, my lived experience? How shall this be decided? I cannot simply resolve to adopt one or another epistemological conception. Is it (critical) realism that is correct, or transcendental philosophy? Aristotle or Kant? How is this 'burning' question of the reality of the external world to be solved (GA56/57: 77–78)?

Epistemology is here presented as providing insights absent from – and meant to overcome – the naïve "slumber" of everyday life. Rather than "clinging to immediate life-experiences," epistemology offers instead a *critical* standpoint that discerns problems where everyday sensibilities had not noticed any. The epistemologist has discovered something that brings the question of the external world to the fore. The discovery concerns the "data" that are genuinely available via experiential processes, in contrast to the conception of the world those data found. Returning to his example of the lectern, Heidegger describes the common starting point for both realism and idealism:

> If, from this [critical] standpoint, I consider the experience of the lectern, it is clear that what is primarily given are sensations, *initially optical* ones, or, if I simultaneously come into physical contact with the lectern, sensations of *touch*. *These data of sense are given*. Up to this

point, the two basic epistemological standpoints, critical *realism* and critical transcendental *idealism*, are in agreement. But now they go off in opposed directions, posing the epistemological question in different ways (GA56/57: 80).

The divergence from this point of agreement is evident in the questions each side then poses. "Critical realism asks, how do I get out of the 'subjective sphere' of sense data to knowledge of the external world?" (GA56/57: 80), whereas "critical transcendental idealism poses the problem: how, remaining within the 'subjective sphere', do I arrive at objective knowledge?" (GA56/57: 80). For Heidegger, the "point of agreement" prior to these questions is the real problem: "The common point of departure of both theories is sense data, whose explanation decides everything" (GA56/57: 84).[38] To see what has gone wrong here, Heidegger returns to the "environmental experience" of the lecture that he first laid out early on in Part II of the lecture course (and which we examined in Section 1.2). Is anything like the epistemologist's sense data really what are "given?" We do not need to review in great detail Heidegger's prior description of seeing the lectern. The main idea that bears upon the present considerations is that there is nothing that is in some way *less* than the lectern that is experientially *prior* to seeing the lectern: "The lectern is given to me immediately in the lived experience of it. I see it as such, I do not see sensations and sense data. I am not conscious of sensations at all" (GA56/57: 85). Heidegger notes that I can, with considerable effort, isolate and concentrate on something answering to the epistemologist's sensations. I might squint and dim down my visual field to try to take in only the lectern's color, for example, thereby inducing a sensation of just brown. In doing so, I *subtract* from my initial and immediate experience. Crucially, with this pared down form of experience, there is no longer the "it worlds" that was evident in the seeing of the lectern: "Do I experience this datum 'brown' as a moment of sensation in the same way that I do the lectern? Does it 'world' in the brown as such, apprehended as a datum? Does my historical 'I' resonate in this apprehension? Evidently not" (GA56/57: 85).

Rather than a discovery, the critical epistemologist has *invented* a problem where there wasn't one by removing everything meaningful about the experience and, once left with a meaningless collection of sensory

---

[38] Heidegger's criticisms here of both critical realism and idealism as demonstrating an equal reliance on a highly problematic – and artificial – notion, sense data, anticipates Merleau-Ponty's later critique of the twin "traditional prejudices" – what he calls *empiricism* and *rationalism* – as likewise working from a shared commitment to sensation as the basic unit of perceptual experience. See Merleau-Ponty (2013: 1–66).

elements, asks how to get from *that* back to the meaningful experience of the lectern. The "meaningful phenomena of environmental experience cannot be explained by destroying their essential character, by denying their real meaning in order to advance a theory. Explanation through dismemberment, i.e. destruction: one wants to explain something which one no longer has as such" (GA56/57: 86). There is, however, nothing obligatory in the critical epistemologist's explanatory ambitions: If meaningless sensory data are not what is immediately present in environmental experience, then determining how to get from such data to "it worlds" is a completely artificial challenge. It is also a hopeless challenge: "When I attempt to explain the environing world theoretically, it collapses upon itself. It does not signify an intensification of experience, or any superior knowledge of the environment, when I attempt its dissolution and subject it to totally unclarified theories and explanations" (GA56/57: 86). Only someone already in the grip of a theory according to which only that kind of sensory data can count as given will be driven to embark on such an explanatory misadventure. Instead, "the genuine solution to the problem of the reality of the external world consists in the insight that this is no problem at all, but rather an absurdity" (GA56/57: 92).

3.2 The Scandal of Philosophy

Consider G. E. Moore's famous response to the problem of the external world, whose persistence Kant had even more famously labeled as "a scandal of philosophy."[39] Moore's response is remarkably straightforward and concise, as it consists of an argument with only two premises and whose conclusion follows with no intermediate steps. All that is needed are gestures toward what Moore characterizes as things "to be met with in space," that is, things residing outside the mind. Mental images, occurrent thoughts, and so on will not suffice, nor will after-images that, even though in some sense appearing in space (hovering in the interval between my face and the far wall, for example), cannot be met with in the right sense. But it is not difficult to find things of the kind Moore has in mind: He needs to look no further than his own two hands (although numerous other "things" would also do the trick). Hence the argument:

 i. Here is one hand
 ii. Here is another hand
 iii. Therefore, there is a world of things external to the mind

---
[39] See Moore (1959). For Kant's "scandal," see Kant (1965: 34).

The skeptic has been refuted, the problem has been solved, and Kant's scandal has been tidily put to rest.

Clear and concise though Moore's argument is, its effectiveness against skepticism is open to question. From an already-skeptical perspective, Moore cannot just help himself to the kinds of premises he uses to launch the argument. In order to be assured of the reality of his two hands, and so be entitled to use them as premises in his argument, Moore must already be assured that there is an external world, a space or realm "outside" the mind within which things like hands can be met. From the skeptic's point of view, the argument will appear thoroughly question-begging. Insistence on the legitimacy of the argument's premises – claiming, for example, that they are obviously true – makes Moore's response to skepticism appear either dogmatic – the skeptic just cannot be right – or, perhaps worse, obtuse in that Moore has not recognized the problem that skepticism poses.[40]

There are moments in Heidegger's explication of being-in-the-world that lend themselves to a Moore-like confrontation with skepticism. Heidegger's assertion that the lectern is "immediately given" in "environmental experience," for example, is apt to sound like one of Moore's premises; the hammer that figures so prominently in Division One of SZ is also a suitable candidate to start Moore's argument. Since I can say, "Here is a lectern" and "Here is a hammer," I can take myself to have thereby demonstrated the reality of the very environing world in which the lectern and hammer can be found. Were this Heidegger's mode of engagement with traditional philosophy, he would be as equally open to the charge of dogmatism or obtuseness as Moore. Heidegger's engagement with skepticism, however, is more subtle and complex than the kind of "defense of common sense" offered by Moore. This is not to say that Heidegger is not occasionally brusque in his handling of challenges to prove the existence of the external world: "The question of whether there is a world at all and whether its being can be proved, makes no sense if it is raised by *Dasein* as being-in-the-world; and who else would raise it?" (SZ: 202). What we need to try to understand is how his saying things along the lines of "world in its most proper sense is just that which is already on hand for any questioning" ((GA20): 294) does not saddle Heidegger with the charge of dogmatism

---

[40] See Chapter III of Stroud (1984) for extensive discussion of Moore's response to skepticism. See also Cerbone (2000). Here and throughout this section, I have profited greatly from Minar (2001), as well as McManus (2013a).

Although Heidegger's saying that world is "already on hand" might sound like a Moore-like assertion, carefully considered, it can be understood as a rebuke to *both* Moore and the skeptic. Start with Moore. Heidegger says that world "is already on hand for any questioning." What holds for questioning holds for *arguing* as well. This suggests a certain kind of belatedness in Moore's attempt at a proof, as the very *meaningfulness* of the premises of the argument render the argument superfluous. Heidegger is not saying here that the premises to Moore's argument are indeed true (although he has no particular reason to doubt them) and that therefore the conclusion to the argument follows. Rather, the argument is, in a sense, upside-down, as it presents the presence of the world as a consequence of there being particular *entities*. The world is *prior to* entities as a space of meaningfulness from out of which particular entities can be *understood*. Heidegger is not dogmatically asserting the existence of particular entities. He is instead asserting only the meaningfulness of the premises, which even the skeptic must grant in order to challenge the argument as question-begging. But if meaning is granted all around, then any debates over the merits of Moore's argument are beside the point. "If Dasein is understood correctly, it defies such proofs, because, in its being, it already *is* what subsequent proofs deem necessary to demonstrate for it" (SZ: 205). What Dasein "already *is*" is being-in-the-world.

Heidegger's appeal to the primacy of world-as-meaningfulness registers what he thinks is an unclarity in the very framing of the problem of the external world: "The world as the 'wherein' of being-in, and the 'world' as entities within-the-world (that in which one is concernfully absorbed) either have been confused or are not distinguished at all" (SZ: 203). Both Moore and the skeptic fixate on the reality of entities – paradigmatically material entities – as the proving ground for the reality of the world. As noted, the inference is from (material) entities to world. The world is here being conceived of as a kind of all-encompassing spatial receptacle. As we have seen throughout our discussion, world in the sense that interests Heidegger is the world of *involvement* rather than *containment*. This is not to say that Heidegger denies the legitimacy of a containing sense of world – it is marked as the first among his four senses of *world* and he never denies its cogency – but only the primacy of it. Our understanding of a containing-sense of world is derivative in relation to – and so parasitic upon – our understanding of world as "the 'wherein' of being-in." We understand the former via the latter and Heidegger sees nothing inherently problematic about any such derivation: "But the world is disclosed essentially *along with the* being of Dasein; with the disclosedness of the world, the 'world' has in each case been discovered too" (SZ: 203). There is, in other words, no *general* problem about "world" in light of Dasein's disclosure of the world.[41]

Kant's Refutation of Idealism[42] – his own attempt to put to an end the scandal of philosophy – accedes to the skeptic's terms and on that basis alone, tries to show that the skeptic can be refuted. What I mean here by the skeptic's terms is that Kant allows the skeptic free use, so to speak, of "inner experiences" – of changes registered as "in me." Kant's argument is that one's ability to *order* those experiences, so that they stand in *temporal* relations of *earlier than, later than*, and *simultaneous* presupposes something *permanent* – an objective temporal order – that Kant reasons must be *outer*. In this way the inner presupposes the outer and the skeptic cannot therefore deny the reality of something external to his experience. In assessing Kant's argument, Heidegger notes at one point that what Kant proves – if we allow that the argument is correct – "is that entities which are changing and entities which are permanent are necessarily present-at-hand together" ((SZ): 204). About this, he remarks that "when two things which are present-at-hand are thus put on the same level, this does not as yet mean that subject and object are present-at-hand together." Kant's error here – his overly generous concession to the skeptic – is to equate an inner process with *experience*, but more needs to be said about any such "process" in order to understand it as illustrating the workings of subjectivity. Such an inner process must not just be arrangeable into a temporal order, but it must – as constituting experience – involve some kind of *meaning*. An ordering of *experiences* would be something along the lines of, "I saw the table *and then* I noticed the bird through the window behind the table and that reminded me to fill the bird feeders." Heidegger's challenge – which Kant allows the skeptic to evade – is how any of *that* is possible without understanding it as founded on – and sustained by – worldly involvement. If Heidegger is right that worldly involvement is prior to – and so founds – meaningful experiences (including any experiences we are wont to characterize as *inner*), then Kant's argument is both unnecessary and misleading: unnecessary because, as noted, Dasein "already is" what proofs deem necessary to demonstrate

---

[41] None of this is to suggest that knowledge of the natural world (and various aspects of human worlds) is *easy*, but that the challenges are just those typically faced by scientists and other inquirers (e.g. historians and economists) in trying to figure out how things work and what is the case. These challenges vary considerably, and so how problems are solved will require different techniques, skills, and forms of ingenuity across different disciplines. There are numerous, particular *problems* of knowledge, but no problem of knowledge *as such*.

[42] See Kant (1965: 244–252).

(involved in a world) and misleading insofar as it depicts our subjectivity as reducible to a meaningless inner process.

Notice here the emergence of the kind of pattern we saw laid down in Heidegger's very early IOP lectures. Heidegger's strategy there was to illustrate the artificiality of the problem of the external world. What generates the appearance of a problem is the characterization of what is immediately present in experience as *sense data,* such that the challenge is to show how to get from *that* to something more robust (such as tables, windows, birds, and bird feeders). In SZ, Heidegger registers a similar complaint: "After the primordial phenomenon of being-in-the-world has been shattered, the isolated subject is all that remains, and this becomes the basis on which it gets joined together with a 'world'" (SZ: 206). We might, however, see him as going further here in the sense that even the idea that we are possessed of sense data is more than the skeptic should be allowed, since identifying a datum as *brown,* for example, or as *rectangular,* already avails itself of worldly sense. Contrary to what he says in the lectures, even bare sensations, if they are meaningfully identified in any way at all, also "world."

3.3 Realism and Idealism

As we saw, in the early IOP lectures, Heidegger traces the problems that beset critical realism and idealism back to a common cause: Their inattention to lived experience in favor of a conception of the "immediately given"[43] determined by antecedent theoretical commitments. Both the realist and the idealist start from the idea that what is given are sense data, discrete sensations that do not initially pertain to anything worldly like lecterns or hammers. Although sense data specifically do not figure much into Heidegger's later discussions of realism and idealism, the idea that prior theoretical commitments lead to a kind of philosophical negligence persists. In *The History of the Concept of Time* lectures, Heidegger emphasizes the need "to extricate the question of the world understood as meaningfulness from a perverse horizon oriented to some theory or other of the reality of the external world or even to an ontology of actuality" (GA20: 293). What fuels epistemology – what lends it a sense of primacy and urgency – is a phenomenologically inadequate ontology. The idea that experience consists of sensations is an especially vivid example of such

---

[43] Indeed, even to think in terms of what is *given* betrays an attitude in the grip of a theory: "'Given' already signifies an inconspicuous but genuine theoretical reflection inflicted upon the environment" (GA56/57: 88–89).

inadequacy, but it is only one example. The kind of neglect Heidegger has in mind runs both wider and deeper:

> When we have seen that the elucidation of the reality of the real is based upon seeing Dasein itself in its basic constitution, then we also have the basic requirement for all attempts to decide between *realism* and *idealism*. In elucidating these positions it is not so much a matter of clearing them up or of finding one or the other to be the solution, but of seeing that both can exist only on the basis of a neglect: they presuppose a concept of 'subject' and 'object' without clarifying these basic concepts with respect to basic composition of Dasein itself. But every serious idealism is in the right to the extent that it sees that being, reality, actuality can be clarified only when being, the real, is present and encountered. Whereas every realism is right to the extent that it attempts to retain Dasein's natural consciousness of the extantness of the world (GA20: 305–306).

While I, following Heidegger's lead, have emphasized the confusions and distortions to which he sees epistemology and epistemology-driven theories as prone, this passage does acknowledge basic – and basically sound – intuitions that lends both realism and idealism their initial attraction and plausibility. Heidegger, however, is careful to acknowledge those intuitions in a way that registers just what each side neglects.[44] Consider first what he sees as right about realism:

> Realism "attempts to retain [Dasein's natural consciousness of] the extantness of the world.

Realism is right insofar as our natural way of being oriented toward much of what populates the world involves the idea of those things being in various ways independent of us. We talk readily of *discovery* when it comes to things such as planets, species of beetles, and subatomic particles, and part of what's built into the idea of discovery is our understanding of such things as being as they are prior to discovering them and regardless of our ever having discovered them. Our discovering them makes them *manifest*, which is not the same as bringing them into existence. Even those items that are not independent of Dasein's projects and purposes – items of equipment such as hammers, screwdrivers, and outboard engines – are not for all that purely *subjective* in the sense of being dependent on being perceived or the like: I don't think of my study – or the house in which it is located – as ceasing to exist when I'm the last person to leave

---

[44] I am indebted to Kate Withy for calling my attention to the way Heidegger's acknowledgment of the intuitions behind realism and idealism carefully incorporates just what each of them neglects.

in the morning (and this is not because I've left the dogs home to keep an eye on things).

What I've placed in brackets registers what Heidegger thinks realism neglects. Realism fixates on what is manifest – in particular, naturally occurring things and processes – while neglecting their *manifestation*. That is not one more naturally occurring process among others, even if it is in some way a naturally occurring process in the sense of being *ontical*. Dasein is ontically distinct from other entities in its being *ontological*, that is, as having an understanding of being. Insofar as it attends to Dasein's understanding at all, as the sequel to this passage makes clear, realism goes entirely wrong in thinking that Dasein's understanding can be construed as a kind of causal process: Realism "falls short in attempting to explain this reality in terms of the real itself, in believing that it can clarify reality by means of a causal process" (GA20: 306). To delineate some things as causal processes and to determine how they work is already to be out amid entities in the world[45] – to have some kind of grip on reality – and so to then try to understand that being amid as itself one more causal process among others is to put the ontical cart before the ontological horse, to understand the understanding of being as one more entity to be understood.

What about the intuition that drives idealism? Heidegger characterizes the right-headed intuition as follows:

> Idealism "is in the right to the extent that it sees that being, reality, actuality can be clarified [only when being, the real, is present and encountered]" (GA20: 305–306).

Idealism rightly calls attention to what realism neglects – our natural consciousness – and in that way underscores how the realist relies on his awareness of things – on things being manifest to him – while focusing only on the things so manifest. Idealism rightly sees that *understanding* constitutes a distinct category whose structure and conditions require a correspondingly distinct sort of account. However, its mistake lies in thinking that that sort of clarification can be accomplished in the absence of what I've placed in brackets above. In other words, it neglects that Dasein's way of being is being-*in-the-world*, and so that understanding can only be clarified insofar as Dasein is not understood as a pure and potentially worldless *subject*, but as already involved with an environing world. With his phenomenology of everydayness, Heidegger's investigation starts with "that

---

[45] Heidegger makes this kind of complaint about "critical realism" in his IOP lectures. See especially GA56/57: 80–82.

understanding of being which belongs already to Dasein and which 'comes alive' in any of its dealing with entities" (SZ: 67). Dasein's "dealing with entities" cannot be bracketed if we want to get this kind of understanding properly into view.

Heidegger's parallel nods – and correctives – toward realism and idealism are not *exactly* parallel, as he accords a greater insight to idealism than to realism. Realism is fixated entirely on *entities*, along with *causal processes* and *mechanisms*, and so is entirely blind[46] to anything such as consciousness, awareness, meaningfulness, and understanding. In *The History of the Concept of Time*, after criticizing realism's fixation on causal processes, he notes about idealism: "Regarded strictly in terms of scientific method, therefore, realism is always at a lower level than every idealism, even when that idealism goes to the extreme of solipsism" (GA20: 306). That even solipsism has the upper hand in relation to realism is a pretty stinging rebuke. In the discussion of these matters in SZ, Heidegger again registers a kind of "doxographic" agreement with realism insofar as he has no wish to "deny that entities within-the-world are present-at-hand" (SZ: 207), but he again laments realism's "lack of ontological understanding," noting that it "tries to explain reality ontically by real connections of interaction between things that are real." Idealism thus "has an advantage in principle over realism."

Heidegger's attempts both to correct and retain elements of realism and idealism find expression in the following passage, which again calls attention to the importance of distinguishing the ontical from the ontological:

> Entities *are*, quite independently of the experience by which they are disclosed, the acquaintance in which they are discovered, and the grasping in which their nature is ascertained. But being 'is' only in the understanding of those entities to whose being something like an understanding of being belongs. Hence being can be something unconceptualized, but it never completely fails to be understood (SZ: 183).

The first sentence of this passage anticipates his "doxographic" agreement with realism later in the chapter, while the second points toward the virtues he sees in idealism. The difficulty this passage poses is how to hold the two ideas Heidegger expresses in the first two sentences together. Why there is a difficulty here can be seen by attending to the first emphasized occurrence of *are*. Heidegger's stress here is meant to underscore the sense of independence he goes on to assert. However, if "being 'is' only in the

---

[46] See GA24: 249 for Heidegger's use of the phrase "blind realism." I discuss this idea in greater detail in Cerbone (2025).

understanding" of Dasein, just how independent are these entities after all? After all, "are" is a form of the verb "to be," and so bound up with the idea of *being*. Doesn't that mean that entities can only *be* what they are insofar as Dasein exists? How can an entity be without being in some way or another? That the sense of independence is attenuated can be seen in a later passage, after Heidegger has remarked on the merits and shortcomings of realism and idealism:

> Of course only as long as Dasein *is* (that is, only as long as an understanding of being is ontically possible), 'is there' being. When Dasein does not exist, 'independence' 'is' not either, nor 'is' the 'in-itself'. In such a case this sort of thing can be neither understood nor not understood. *In such a case* it cannot be said that entities are, nor can it be said that they are not. But *now*, as long as there is an understanding of being and therefore an understanding of the present-at-hand, it can indeed be said that *in this case* entities will still continue to be (SZ: 212).

Read in the light of this passage, the realistic sounding assertions of independence in the prior passage are qualified considerably, as even the idea of an entity being independent – being as it is regardless of what we make of it – still depends on there being Dasein. There thus appears to be a kind of meta-dependence that takes back the initial claim to independence. Some readers of SZ have tried to wave away this appearance. Taylor Carman ascribes to Heidegger an "ontical realism," whose central commitment is to the idea that present-at-hand "entities exist and have a determinate structure in the absence of any and all views, period" (Carman 2003: 167). Despite the case-closed tone of Carman's characterization, if the absence of "any and all views" is another way of describing the absence of Dasein, then it would appear that the case needs to be reopened: Having a determinate structure – even an "independent" determinate structure – still depends upon Dasein. In other words, Carman's ontic realism runs afoul of what Heidegger says about the "in such a case" of there being no Dasein: If it can neither be said that entities are, nor that they are not in such a case, in what sense can entities have a "determinate structure" if there is no Dasein? Entities can have a determinate structure only if they *are*, but that's among the things that Heidegger says cannot be said. Other readers[47] have opted for a more modest *minimal realism* that foregoes the idea of determinate structure, leaving only the notion of a bare *something* – call it THE REAL – that is independent of Dasein (and which is accessible

---

[47] See Hoffman (2000) and Kochan (2017) for a conception of Heideggerian realism along these lines. I question this conception in Cerbone (2025).

to Dasein through moody, noncognitive affective episodes). Paring back does not really seem to help matters: *Being* undifferentiated is still a way for something to be, and so would still seem to depend on Dasein; moreover, what philosophers want when they are attracted to realism is generally something more robust and informative than a bare and barren sense of THE REAL.

The problem here is that what Heidegger says at the ontical level – what leads Carman to characterize his view as *ontical realism* – appears *threatened* rather than *bolstered* at the ontological level. The way Heidegger characterizes these two levels and their interplay would appear to transpose into his ontical-ontological idiom Kant's prior distinction between *empirical* realism and *transcendental* idealism. For Kant, we can with some right consider objects as existing independently of us, as existing "out there" in space and time; however, since space and time themselves are the *a priori* forms of intuition and so must be understood as features of our minds rather than as real in and of themselves, those independently existing objects are mind-dependent after all.[48] They are, one and all, *appearances*, while knowledge of what Kant calls things-in-themselves is impossible. William Blattner has, more than any other contemporary reader of SZ, emphasized the Kantian legacy in Heidegger's handling of realism and idealism. While Blattner allows that Heidegger may be some kind of ontical realist, he is an ontological idealist – an idealist about being[49] – which again undermines the air of finality in Carman's statement of ontical realism.

It would be too much to try to adjudicate these disputes here.[50] An underlying problem with these arguments is that they do not take seriously – or seriously enough – Heidegger's ambition of breaking free from – or overcoming – *both* realism and idealism. To marshal passages that lend credence to the idea that he is a realist or the opposite only suggests that we have not yet taken to heart the radicality of Heidegger's stance with

---

[48] For a reading of Kant that sees what he says at the transcendental level as canceling what he says at the empirical level, see Chapter IV of Stroud (1984). As Stroud reads Kant – including his response to "the scandal of philosophy" – Kant does not succeed in refuting skepticism, but instead offers an account of empirical knowledge that ultimately vindicates the skeptic.

[49] More precisely, Blattner reads Heidegger as a *temporal* idealist – an idealist about time – and since temporality is the horizon of being, he is an ontological idealist derivatively. But even without attending to the intricacies of Heidegger's views on time in Division Two, for Blattner, that he is an ontological idealist is already evident in these Division One passages. See Blattner (1994); Blattner (2004); and Blattner (2005).

[50] I have weighed in on these matters more than once elsewhere: Cerbone (1995); Cerbone (2007); and Cerbone (2025).

respect to traditional philosophy. Either that, or that we ultimately think that Heidegger was not nearly as radical as he sought to be, as his views can still be located in a familiar constellation of possible positions. To see how and why we might refrain from doing so, consider again Heidegger's accordance of the upper hand to idealism. In his 1927 Basic Problems of Phenomenology lectures, he notes that his insistence on the primacy of *world*, understood in terms of meaningfulness, is apt to be understood as introducing a subjective element, thereby inviting the charge of idealism. Remarking on this, he notes that "we have to ask what this idealism – which today is feared almost like the foul fiend incarnate – really is searching for" (GA24: 238). What idealism is searching for is what Heidegger takes himself to have found in the interrelation between Dasein and world: Dasein is worldly through and through, but what is worldly reflects Dasein's modes of understanding. The latter bit of this should appease the idealist, given its emphasis on understanding. But, is the former bit enough to appease the realist?

Consider again Carman's appeal to "determinate structure" in his characterization of ontical realism. I remarked before that his case-closed tone was markedly premature in light of Heidegger's remarks about the way the dependence of being on Dasein qualifies considerably his assertion that entities *are* "quite independently of the experience by which they are disclosed," and so on. To open the case further, we might ask here just *what* determinate structure the ontical realist has in mind here. Moreover, we might ask just *how* those determinations were made. Did this determinate structure simply impress itself upon Dasein's understanding, as though it could not but arrive at things having just *that* structure? Again, this begins to veer close to understanding understanding as the outcome of a kind of causal process: The way the world – or here, really, 'world' – is structured (in-itself) causes Dasein to understand the world as being so-structured. The force behind Heidegger's condemnation of "blind realism" (GA24: 249) should be evident here, as what realism is blind to is the kind of *work* that had to be done to determine any of this determinative structure. It is not as though we just open our eyes – or open our minds – and the material world stamps its structure upon them. What structure we *take* the material world to have reflects the ways in which we have investigated it, the interests that have guided those investigations, the skills and techniques brought to bear, the models and theories we have drawn up and tested. At the same time, of course, all of this *activity* is not the work of an isolated, worldless *subject*, but of a being always already at grips with its world, and, by extension, the 'world.' This is – or should be – realistic *enough* to appease all but the blindest realist without throwing in with the "foul fiend."

4 Beyond *Being and Time*

4.1 Pathways

Despite its status and stature – both within Heidegger's overall corpus and for twentieth-century philosophy more generally – SZ was never advertised as complete or definitive. Its two published divisions were to be followed by a third, and these three together were only to have been Part One of a two-part work (the second part was likewise to consist of three divisions). Although Heidegger's promissory notes were partially cashed in his writings and lectures in the late 1920s, the work was never finished in the way Heidegger initially envisioned. Moreover, had the work been completed, it would have only further underscored the role Division One of Part One was always described as playing, namely, that it was to serve as a *preparatory* analysis. As preparatory, Heidegger's characterizations there of Dasein's being-in-the-world should not be considered the final word on the matter. Heidegger is clear about this in work immediately following the publication of SZ in 1927, especially in his essay *On the Essence of Ground* (OEG) and his lecture course, *The Fundamental Concepts of Metaphysics*. In both works, he revisits what he refers to as *the problem of world*. In doing so, he situates the account of being-in-the-world developed in SZ in a manner that reinforces its preliminary status.

At the outset of the second part of the FCM lectures, Heidegger takes up the question, "What is world?" and delineates three "paths" to approaching the question (he cautions that these are not the only three). His numbering of the paths does not align with the order of their appearance in his writings, as he cites as first a path he follows in OEG. This is a "historical path" where "we pay close attention to the word and pursue the *history of the word* 'world' and the historical development of the concept it contains" (GA29/30: 261). We will return to this historical approach shortly. The path laid down in SZ does not attend at all to the history of the word "world" (indeed, Heidegger does little to motivate the fourfold taxonomy he offers). Instead, looking back, he describes himself as having "attempted in *Being and Time* to provide a preliminary characterization of the *phenomenon of world* by interpreting the *way in which we at first and for the most part move about in our everyday world*" (GA29/30: 262). Although Heidegger in OEG and the FCM lectures does not disown his prior account of Dasein in its everydayness, in both works he nonetheless flags that account as being potentially misleading. What is misleading about it is that it encourages a conception of world as equivalent to the kinds of referential totalities he describes in Division One via examples of workshops and the like. These certainly appear to be *worlds* in his third sense of the four he offers in SZ. As we noted in Section 2.3, however, worlds in this sense, as taking the indefinite article (*a* world) and allowing pluralization, threaten to obscure from view any notion of *the* world, as well as the idea that Dasein's *transcendence* is toward world in that richer sense: "If indeed one identifies the ontic contexture of items of utility, or equipment, with world and interprets being-in-the-world as dealing with items of utility, then there is certainly no prospect of any understanding of transcendence as being-in-the-world in the sense of the 'fundamental constitution of Dasein'" (GA9: 155, Note 55). Staying local misses the point entirely: "In and through this initial characterization of the phenomenon of world the task is to press on and point out the phenomenon of world as a problem. It never occurred to me, however, to try and claim or prove with this interpretation that the essence of man consists in the fact that he knows how to handle knives and forks or use the tram" (GA29/30: 263). This is not to say that Heidegger had not started to "press on" already in SZ to "the phenomenon of the world as a problem." Indeed in § 69c – toward the end of Division Two – he takes up the problem of transcendence, asking the question of "how anything like the world in its unity with Dasein is ontologically possible" (SZ: 364). Heidegger's discussion here is brief – roughly three pages – and he vacillates between talk of *a* world and *the* world: Dasein is an entity for whom "something like a world ... has been disclosed" (SZ: 365) and "Dasein *is* essentially 'in a world'" (SZ: 365), but also that "the [NB: not *a*] world is, as it were, already 'further outside' than any object can ever be" (SZ: 366). This appeal to the world as being "further outside" points toward the idea of transcendence. It is not surprising, then, that *transcendence* figures prominently in both of the post-SZ paths Heidegger follows. Indeed, in OEG, Heidegger declares transcendence to be definitive of being-in-the-world: "We name *world* that *toward which* Dasein as such transcends, and shall now determine transcendence as *being-in-the-world*" (GA9: 139).[51]

In this final section, we will examine more closely this appeal to transcendence, both as it figures in the historical path traced in OEG, as well as the third path he follows in the FCM lectures. That third path – described as a "comparative analysis" – revisits and qualifies considerably ideas

---

[51] Transcendence figures prominently in GA26, which he draws upon in *The Essence of Reasons*; see especially § 11.

broached in his Aristotle lectures of 1924 concerning how to understand the manner in – and extent to – which animals *have* a world and how that sense of having differs fundamentally from Dasein's having of world.

4.2 Transcendence and World

Before embarking on his historical investigation of the concept of world in OEG, Heidegger first notes how, pre-philosophically, the idea of *the world* simply equates to the idea of *all there is*. When we talk about the *whole world*, we simply mean *everything*. However, if being-in-the-world were keyed to *this* notion of world, it would only mean that Dasein – as being-in-the-world – is in the midst of entities. Heidegger observes that "this is in the end the emptiest and most trivial thing that can be said" (GA9: 140). Moreover, it does nothing to pick out anything distinctive about human existence, as anything that is – insofar as it is – can be found amid everything else that is. Being-in-the-world, on this construal, picks out nothing essential about Dasein. Every entity is in some way amid other entities, but most entities are not oriented toward other entities in the sense of those entities being *manifest* to them. The desk in my study is there alongside the chair I use to sit at it, as well as bookcases, a rug, and so on, but my desk is in no way aware of the chair that I use nor of anything else. All of these things are, however, manifest to me, which means that I understand them and comport myself toward them in meaningful ways (meaningfulness is again the key idea: my desk means something to me, but nothing means anything to the desk). Moreover, my understanding – my awareness of things – is not limited to my study and what populates it; rather, my understanding extends indefinitely outward. This is not to say that I understand everything there is – there's lots I don't understand – but I understand even those things that I don't understand as among everything there is. Dasein is thus not just among other beings, but is oriented toward other beings as belonging to a totality. That form of orientation gives us a glimmer of what Heidegger means by transcendence: "Human Dasein – a being that finds itself situated *in the midst* of beings, comporting itself *toward* beings – in doing so exists in such a way that beings are always manifest as a whole" (GA9: 156). As he is careful to note, "This wholeness is understood without the whole of those beings that are manifest being explicitly grasped or indeed 'completely' investigated in their specific connections, domains, and layers" (GA9: 156).

Dasein's transcendence is a matter of its distinctive form of understanding (what is distinctive about it will be more clearly delineated by contrasting it with animalistic forms of understanding – this is the topic of the comparative analysis of the FCM lectures). "Yet the understanding of this wholeness, an understanding that in each case reaches ahead and embraces it, is a surpassing in the direction of world" (GA9: 156). As surpassing, this form of understanding is not oriented toward something outside of – or not of – the world, but should be thought of as reaching round and taking in the world as a whole. Heidegger's "necessarily fragmented" investigation of the concept of world, which begins with Heraclitus and ends with Kant, presents that history as groping toward this understanding of transcendence and world. "In the case of such elementary concepts, the ordinary meaning is usually not the originary and essential one. The latter is repeatedly covered over, and attains its conceptual articulation only rarely and with difficulty" (GA9: 142). Nonetheless, glimpses of this "constantly hidden" meaning can be had. I will not try here to recount the several historical fragments Heidegger pieces together. I will note only the first two particular but especially important links in that historical chain that already involve a twofold sense of "world" that gestures toward transcendence.

Heidegger begins his historical account with the pre-Socratic Greeks, among them Heraclitus, whose Fragment # 89 – "The wakeful have one single cosmos that is common to all, while in sleep each man turns away from this world into his own" – illustrates the complex sense of *world*. Present already in the Greek notion of *kosmos* is an understanding of world as more than a mere aggregate or collection of everything that happens to exist. "World" refers to the *how* – the manner – of things existing, as belonging to the world – this world – and not another (possible) world. Moreover, Heraclitus' fragment already signals something distinctively human: The wakeful *have* a common world and understand that world as held in common. Even for the ancient Greeks, Heidegger claims, the world "belongs precisely to human Dasein, even though it embraces in its whole all beings, including Dasein" (GA9: 143). With the emergence of Christianity, "the relation between *kosmos* and human Dasein" becomes "sharper and clearer" (GA9: 143). In one sense, "world" refers again to all that is, now understood as God's Creation, but "world" takes on a further meaning keyed to human existence to mark out a sinful worldliness in contrast to being oriented toward God. As fallen, human existence is of the world in the sense of loving the world rather than what is divine. (Other creatures belong to the world in the first sense, but they are not worldly in the second sense.) In the Gospel of John, for example, "world designates the fundamental form of human Dasein removed from God, the *character of being human* pure and simple" (GA9: 144).

The problem of world can be understood as the problem of the interplay of these two dimensions: Worldliness is a human phenomenon that takes account of beings as a whole. World in the more pedestrian sense of all that exists is not in any way a defective concept, but it does not capture their being manifest – and how they are manifest – to human understanding. Human worlds – in the plural – are ways of making sense of everything there is. Unlike workshops and executive suites – the world of carpentry and the business world – that are, we might say, bounded totalities,[52] worldliness in the sense that Heidegger is after is *unbounded*. Being-in-the-world refers to this orientation toward this unbounded form of understanding. In being so oriented, Heidegger says that Dasein "forms" the world:

> This occurrence of a projective casting-over, in which the being of Dasein is temporalized, is being-in-the-world. 'Dasein transcends' means: in the essence of its being it is *world-forming*, 'forming' in the multiple sense that it lets world occur, and through the world gives itself an original view (form). That is not explicitly grasped, yet functions precisely as a paradigmatic form for all manifest beings, among which each respective Dasein also belongs (GA9: 158).

A human world is something *formed*, not in the sense of something deliberately made, but as tied to the way things are understood by Dasein. What is formed is *an original view* or a *model* that encompasses, however implicitly, all that there is. A human world is a way of making sense of everything – no world leaves anything out – even while being only one world among other possible worlds. The Christian world, for example, provides a view on everything there is, as God's Creation, as reflecting God's goodness, but as lesser in relation to what is divine. That world, which Heidegger associates with Medieval Christianity, is no longer up and running in the way it was in the Middle Ages. That view of things has waned as new worlds have been formed. Notice that we are here still availing ourselves of the indefinite article – the Christian world is *a* world – and the plural – there have been, and will be, numerous human worlds – while nonetheless including a sense of *the world*: What makes these worlds *worlds* – what their *worlding* consists in – is their orientation toward the totality of what is, what Heidegger in the FCM lectures refers to as "beings as such and

---

[52] As we saw in Sections 1.3 and 2.3, such "local" worlds are what Heidegger calls permeable. While totalities in some sense, they are not self-contained but always refer beyond themselves. Considered carefully, such examples of worlds already point toward the problem of world that Heidegger takes up after *Being and Time*.

as a whole." Heidegger talks there too of world-formation in unfolding his comparative analysis. To those lectures we now turn.

4.3 Animality and World-Formation

Recall that in his 1924 Aristotle lectures, Heidegger notes that "an animal is not simply moving down the road, pushed along by some mechanism. It is in the world in the sense of having it" (GA18: 18). Unlike water that flows in a river or a rock that breaks loose from the side of a cliff, the animal *moves itself* and its movements are *purposive* in that we describe the animal as, variously, *seeking* shelter, *hunting* for prey, *hiding* from predators, and so on. Heidegger's remarks on animality in his FCM lectures five years later preserve some of what he marked out previously as distinctive of animals. The animal is not to be understood as *worldless* like a stone, but Heidegger's later understanding of the animal as *having* a world is far more qualified and restricted. Within his threefold comparative analysis, whereas the stone is worldless and human beings are *world-forming*, the animal is *poor in world*. In the 1924 lectures, Heidegger had marked a sharp distinction between human and animal forms of being-in-the-world, since only the human way of being-in-the-world involved *language*. Something quite like that marker carries over into the later lectures, but the ramifications of the animal's lack of language – its lacking *logos* – are now more severe in terms of attenuating the animal's form of *having*, so much so that *being-in-the-world* is not applicable to animals.

Consider the following passage from the FCM lectures:

> The woodworm, for example, which bores into the bark of the oak tree is encircled by *its own* specific ring. But the woodworm itself, and that means together with this encircling ring of its own, finds itself in turn within the ring encircling the woodpecker as it looks for the worm. And the woodpecker finds itself in all this within the ring encircling the squirrel which startles it as it works. Now this whole context of openness within the range of captivation encircling the animal realm is not merely characterized by an enormous wealth of contents and relations which we can hardly imagine, but in all of this it is still fundamentally different from the manifestness of being as encountered in the world-forming Dasein of man (GA29/30: 401).

Notice in particular Heidegger's appeals to *encirclement* and *captivation* in describing the life of the animal. To say that the animal is "encircled by *its own* specific ring," which involves a "range of captivation" does not mean that the animal is held captive in the same manner as when it is kept in a cage. The animals Heidegger here describes *move freely*, but their movements, activities, and sensory capacities operate within a predetermined range in accordance with the kinds of animal they are. Animal activity and perception involves an often very complicated array of *inhibitors* and *disinhibitors*, what we might loosely think of as *triggers* that incite and extinguish in the animal various kinds of response. The squirrel that startles the woodpecker, for example, spends a great deal of its time gathering acorns: acorns trigger gathering – as well as eating and storing – on the part of the squirrel, which is as much as to say that acorns are *food* for the squirrel. Acorns trigger a food response from the squirrel, whereas the woodworm that the woodpecker seeks does not. While from a purely objective point of view, the woodworm is a part of the squirrel's surroundings, it is not within the squirrel's encirclement. Nothing about woodworms triggers any kind of response from the squirrel. Various animals have various kinds of often exquisitely tuned triggers. An owl, for example, might be triggered to fly in a particular direction by the very faint sound of a rodent scurrying through the leaves, while wolves and other predators can locate prey by scents that barely register – if at all – to the human sense of smell. Despite having such exquisitely attuned mechanisms, different kinds of animals will often not be triggered at all by sounds and smells that are abundantly present in the sense of being at a volume or intensity well within the range of what that animal can in some circumstances pick up. My dogs, for example, whose range of hearing is far greater than mine, do not react *at all* to loud music in the kitchen when they are keeping me company as I clean up (by contrast, they react excitedly to plates put down on the floor to "pre-wash"). Unless a stretch of the music includes dogs barking or resembles footsteps on gravel or knocks on a door, the music does not register for my dogs. They seem not to hear it at all, unless or until a sound like one that has significance in their canine circle happens to sound.

What I've described thus far is apt to trigger a response of its own: Aren't human beings also animals with sensory capacities that are only operative in a particular range? Don't we have a "circle" of our own that captivates us just as the squirrel is captivated by its circle and so on? While it is true that human beings enjoy only a limited sensory range – some sounds are beyond the reach of human ears and the same goes for sights and smells – we are not *confined* to our sensory range in the manner of the animal: The animal hears what it hears in that it is attuned to – and triggered by – some sounds but not others, but *nothing else* is manifest to the animal as a *possible* sound or *possible* sight. Consider again the example of food: The acorn triggers a food response in the squirrel, while the woodworm does not. The squirrel responds foodishly, so to speak, to the acorns but not to the woodworm. In so responding, it does not see or otherwise register the woodworm as *not food for squirrels*, nor does it see or otherwise register the woodworm as *possibly food* for other kinds of creatures. The squirrel is captivated by its "encircling ring" in that it has no sense – no conception – of there being anything *beyond* the array of what triggers its activity. The squirrel does not – and cannot – conceive of what it responds to as only possible responses that *could be otherwise*. Whereas notice what I've done in the preceding paragraphs: I've picked out – however roughly – what is edible for a squirrel in contrast to what is edible for a woodpecker, what is audible to an owl, and what is smellable by a wolf. This is not just to say that the woodpecker, owl, and wolf figure into my "circle," but that my understanding *transcends* any kind of encirclement. I am not *confined* to what I can hear or see or smell, as I can understand the *possibility* of sounds that I cannot hear and things that I cannot see. Human beings can also build instruments to bring those things within the range of our sensory capacities: cameras with infrared sensors, microphones, amplifiers, and so on. That kind of activity would make no sense if we were not open to the possibility of sounds and images beyond the range of our unaided hearing and seeing.

It's not just that a squirrel, upon seeing a woodworm, is not able to think, "I bet that woodpecker over there would like to eat this," but that there's a very real sense in which the squirrel does not register the presence of the woodworm *at all*, at least certainly not *as* a woodworm. I don't eat woodworms. I don't know if they even count as edible for human beings. But I still might take note of a woodworm, on a hike for example. I can look at the woodworm without its "triggering" any particular response from me. I can look at the woodworm just to look at it, to note its wriggling and the structure of its body. I can see it *as* distinctively marked by ringed segments. I can, as noted, see it as food for the woodpecker whose nearby pecking I hear, and not as food for the squirrel that just scampered away. I can also see it *as* the creature that's responsible for these marks on the oak tree where I first spotted it. In seeing it that way, I can also see it as responsible for the blight that's affecting oak trees in my region, and so as something I should consider killing rather than putting back onto the tree where I found it. I can see it as wiggling and wriggling in a way that reminds me of twirling spaghetti onto a fork. And so on. The availability of the *as* is central to Heidegger's reflections on the question, "What is world?" In keeping with his earlier remarks on transcendence, the *as* that is the mark of world is the "as" in *as such* and in *as a whole*: "World is not the totality of beings, is not the accessibility of beings as such, not the manifestness of beings as such that lies at the basis of this accessibility – world is rather the *manifestness of beings as such as a whole*" (GA29/30: 412). The various uses of *as* noted earlier in my examining the woodworm indicate what he refers to here as the "accessibility of beings as such," and so points the way toward the grounding sense of manifestness. Human beings are world-forming in that beings are manifest: to be manifest *as such as a whole* is to appear against a horizon of possibilities, rather than rigidly determined in one particular way. Such rigidity is the mark of the animal's captivation, its being triggered by the presence of things rather than open to them just as what they are and can be.

Trivial though the example of looking at a worm may be, that I can see freely in myriad different ways is grounded in transcendence. Heidegger explicitly connects freedom and transcendence. Transcendence "consists in freedom" (GA9: 164), and more emphatically: "*Freedom alone can let a world prevail and let it world for Dasein.* World never *is*, but *worlds*" (GA9: 164). Call it beginner's luck or consider it one full revolution of the hermeneutic circle: Either way, Heidegger was clearly already on to something all the way back in 1919.

5 Concluding Remarks: Further Beyond *Being and Time*

Although Section 4 ventured beyond SZ to examine some of the ways in which Heidegger modified and developed the concept of being-in-the-world in subsequent work, that discussion ventured only as far as 1930. Of course, Heidegger's philosophical thinking and writing do not stop at that point, far from it, as he lived until 1976 and continued to write and lecture for much of that time. Stopping at 1930 was not an arbitrary decision on my part, nor just a matter of the limitations imposed by the *Elements* format. The writings examined in Section 4 remain in the orbit of SZ. Although SZ remains a kind of touchstone throughout Heidegger's philosophical thinking, his later understanding of its significance is filtered considerably through the many changes his thinking undergoes after the early 1930s. While not a decisive break, the "turn"[53] in his thinking is sufficient for it to be commonplace to distinguish between an *early* Heidegger and a *later* Heidegger, even while scholars wrangle over how best to understand the distinction (that it is also becoming commonplace to distinguish a *middle* Heidegger is one indication of such wrangling). This is not the

---

[53] See Braver (2021) for a concise account of the idea of a *turn* in Heidegger's philosophy.

place to consider the nuances of the distinction between the early and later Heidegger, nor to wade into the disputes to which that distinction has given rise. I want, more modestly, only to gesture toward a small handful of later developments that bear most directly upon the idea of being-in-the-world, drawing primarily from his essay, "The Origin of the Work of Art" (OWA), which was first drafted in the mid-1930s, and also briefly touching upon ideas found in later essays. That there is more to say goes without saying.

That Heidegger in OWA ventures an account of the nature and role of works of art as a distinct category already indicates a movement beyond the SZ tripartite ontology of *Dasein*, the *ready-to-hand*, and the *present-at-hand*. Indeed, Heidegger devotes considerable attention to distinguishing artworks from equipment. The details of Heidegger's account cannot concern us here. What is important for our purposes is the way the essay marks out two significant changes in Heidegger's thinking about the notion of *world*: first, a radical historicization of world (premonitions of which are already apparent in his talk of "world-formation" in OEG and FCM) and, second, a pairing of the concept of world with a new notion of *earth*.

That Heidegger distinguishes among different historical worlds was already evident in SZ – as our discussion of Section 2. X illustrates – but in the framework of SZ, the differences among various historical worlds may be largely regarded as ontical variations of an ontological structure that can itself be ahistorically described. Different worlds have different arrays of equipment (spears and swords here, longbows and muskets there), but these are different ontical fillings-in of the ontological structure that includes the ready-to-hand. Heidegger's account in OWA radicalizes this historicality insofar as it considers worlds within a broader shift to a more historical and epochal *history of being*. Historical worlds on this new account embody different – and largely incommensurable[54] – *understandings of being*. Historical worlds, which "gather" the "paths and relations" of human communal life (GA5: 27–28), are distinct – and finite[55] – "openings" within which things are manifest in accordance with the kind of gathering definitive of that world: The world of the ancient Greeks, for example, involves a radically

---

[54] That Heidegger regards different historical worlds as in many ways incommensurable complicates what I referred to in Section 2 as the *accessibility* of worlds from and to one another. However, it is important to note that even if aspects of one historical world are opaque from the perspective of another, the former is still accessible *as a world* from the standpoint of the latter.

[55] See White (2009) for a reading of Heidegger that argues that his interest in finitude and death applies primarily to worlds rather than to individual people. White's reading quite explicitly reads Heidegger "backwards," that is, she reads *SZ* in light of the later work.

different understanding of being (roughly, that being equals *physis*, the upsurge of nature) than, say, the world of the Medieval Christians, where everything is manifest as expressing the plans and purposes of God. In the world of the ancient Greeks, there cannot *be* saints and sinners, just as for the Medieval Christians, the heroes celebrated by the ancient Greeks would be only overly proud sinners.

Notice that Heidegger's newly radicalized historicism preserves the idea of the plurality of worlds that we considered in Section 2.3. In giving new emphasis to the historicality of worlds, Heidegger ascribes more importance to the way different historical worlds are *sited*, that is, as founded upon and making sense of a specific locale or region. The site-specific character of historical worlds points toward the interplay between *world* and *earth*. "World is grounded on earth, and earth rises up through world" (GA5: 95). *Earth* for Heidegger includes the idea of the literal ground upon which a historical is founded; the particulars of that ground's earthiness dictate what that world must do to reach an accommodation with its environs. There is thus for Heidegger a kind of *struggle* between earth and world. Less literally, we can think of this struggle in terms of sense-making: A world is a way of making sense of things that strives for maximal comprehension – every world tries to leave nothing out – but earth marks the resistance to that striving: "The earth is openly illuminated as itself only where it is apprehended and preserved as the essentially undisclosable, as that which withdraws from any disclosure, in other words, keeps itself constantly closed up" (GA5: 33).

Earth figures centrally as well in Heidegger's even later appeal – in essays such as "Building, Dwelling, Thinking" (GA7: 145–164) and "The Thing" (GA7: 165–188) – to the notion of a *fourfold* of *earth*, *sky*, *mortals*, and *divinities*.[56] The interplay of these four dimensions, which Heidegger describes as *mirroring* one another, corresponds in large part to what he had earlier described in terms of *world*: The fourfold constitutes a kind of site of significance to which human beings are receptive and responsive (rather than fully responsible). Heidegger describes this receptivity and responsiveness as *dwelling*. Dwelling – the distinctive way in which mortals (going proxy for Dasein) are involved in the fourfold – can thus be seen as a reconfiguration of being-in-the-world.

---

[56] See Wrathall (2021b). There, Wrathall connects the later idea of the fourfold to Heidegger's earlier talk of the worlding of the world.

References

Works by Heidegger

SZ — *Sein und Zeit.* Tübingen: Niemeyer, 1967. English translation: *Being and Time.* Translated by J. Macquarrie & E. Robinson. New York: Harper Collins, 1962.

GA5 — *Holzwege. Gesamtausgabe*, Volume 5. Edited by F.-W. von Herrmann. Frankfurt: Klostermann, 1977. English Translation: *Off the Beaten Track.* Edited by J. Young and K. Haynes. Cambridge: Cambridge University Press, 202.

GA7 — *Vorträge und Aufsätze. Gesamtausgabe*, Volume 7. Edited by F.-W. von Herrmann. Frankfurt: Klostermann, 2002. Partial English translation: *Poetry, Language, Thought.* Edited by A. Hofstadter. New York: Harper and Row, 1971.

GA9 — *Wegmarken. Gesamtausgabe*, Volume 9. Edited by F.-W. von Herrmann. Frankfurt: Klostermann, 1976. English translation: *Pathmarks.* Edited by W. McNeill. Cambridge: Cambridge University Press, 1998.

GA18 — *Grundbegriffe der aristotelischen Philosophie. Gesamtausgabe*, Volume 18. Edited by M. Michalski. Frankfurt: Klostermann, 2002. English translation: *Basic Concepts of Aristotelian Philosophy.* Translated by R. D. Metcalf & M. B. Tanzer. Bloomington: Indiana University Press, 2009.

GA20 — *Prolegomena zur Geschichte des Zeitbegriffs. Gesamtausgabe*, Volume 20. Edited by P. Jaeger. Frankfurt: Klostermann, 1979. English translation: *History of the Concept of Time: Prolegomena.* Translated by T. Kisiel. Bloomington: Indiana University Press, 1985.

GA24 — *Der Grundprobleme der Phänomenologie. Gesamtausgabe*, Volume 24. Edited by F.-W. von Herrmann. Frankfurt: Klostermann, 1989 (Zweite Auflage). English translation:

GA26 — *Metaphysische Anfangsgründe der Logik im Ausgang von Leibniz. Gesamtausgabe*, Voume 26. Edited by K. Held. Frankfurt: Kolstermann, 1978. English translation: *The Metaphysical Foundations of Logic.* Translated by M. Heim. Bloomington: Indiana University Press, 1984.

GA29/30 — *Die Grundbegriffe der Metaphysik: Welt, Endlichkeit, Einsamkeit. Gesamtausgabe*, Volume 29/30. Edited by F.-W. von Herrmann.

Frankfurt: Klostermann, 1983. English translation: *The Fundamental Concepts of Metaphysics: World, Finitude, Solitude*. Translated by W. McNeill & N. Walker. Bloomington: Indiana University Press, 1995.

GA56/57   *Zur Bestimmung der Philosophie. Gesamtausgabe*, Volume 56/57. Edited by B. Heimbüchel. Frankfurt: Klostermann, 1987. English translation: *Towards the Definition of Philosophy*. Translated by T. Sadler. London: Continuum, 2000.

GA58   *Grundprobleme der Phänomenologie (1919/1920). Gesamtausgabe*, Volume 58. Edited by H.-H. Gander. Frankfurt: Klostermann, 1993. English translation: *Basic Problems of Phenomenology*. Translated by S. Campbell. London: Bloomsbury, 2013.

GA63   *Ontologie (Hermeneutik der Faktizität). Gesamtausgabe*, Volume 63. Edited by K. Bröcker-Oltmanns. Frankfurt: Klostermann, 1988. English translation: *Ontology – The Hermeneutics of Facticity*. Translated by J. van Buren. Bloomington: Indiana University Press, 1999.

Other Works

Blattner, William (1994) "Is Heidegger a Kantian Idealist?" *Inquiry* 37 (2): 185–201.

(2004) "Heidegger's Kantian Idealism Revisited." *Inquiry* 47 (4): 321–337.

(2005) *Heidegger's Temporal Idealism*. Cambridge: Cambridge University Press.

(2023) *Heidegger's "Being and Time."* London: Bloomsbury.

Braver, Lee (2021) "Turn." In *The Heidegger Lexicon*, edited by M. Wrathall. Cambridge: Cambridge University Press.

Burch, Matthew (2013) "The Existential Sources of Phenomenology: Heidegger on Formal Indication." *European Journal of Philosophy* 21 (2): 258–278.

Carman, Taylor (2003) *Heidegger's Analytic*. Cambridge: Cambridge University Press.

Cerbone, David R. (1995) "World, World-Entry, and Realism in Early Heidegger." *Inquiry* 38 (4): 401–421.

(2000) "Proofs and Presuppositions." In *Heidegger, Authenticity and Modernity*, edited by M. Wrathall and J. Malpas. Cambridge: The MIT Press.

(2007) "Heidegger on Realism and Truth." In *A Companion to Heidegger*, edited by H. Dreyfus and M. Wrathall. Oxford: Blackwell.

(2025) "Heidegger's Evenhanded Approach to Realism and Idealism." In *The Cambridge Critical Guide to* Being and Time, edited by A. Wendland and T. Keiling. Cambridge: Cambridge University Press.

Dahlstrom, Daniel (1994) "Heidegger's Method: Philosophical Concepts as Formal Indications." *The Review of Metaphysics* 47 (4): 775–795.

Dreyfus, Hubert (1991) *Being-in-the-World*. Cambridge: The MIT Press.

Guignon, Charles (1983) *Heidegger and the Problem of Knowledge*. Indianapolis, IN: Hackett.

Hägglund, Martin (2019) *This Life*. New York: Random House.

Haugeland, John (2013) *Dasein Disclosed*. Cambridge: Harvard University Press.

Hoffman, Piotr (2000) "Heidegger and the Problem of Idealism." *Inquiry* 43 (4): 403–411.

Kant, Immanuel (1965) *Critique of Pure Reason*. Translated by Norman Kemp-Smith. New York: St. Martin's.

Keiling, Tobias (2023) "Worlds, Worlding." *Epoché* 27 (2): 273–295.

Kisiel, Theodore (1995) *The Genesis of Heidegger's Being and Time*. Berkeley: University of California Press.

Kochan, Jeff (2017) *Science as Social Existence: Heidegger and the Sociology of Scientific Knowledge*. Cambridge: Open Book Publishers.

Martin, Wayne (2013) "The Semantics of 'Dasein' and the Modality of *Being and Time*." In *The Cambridge Companion to Heidegger's* Being and Time, edited by M. Wrathall. Cambridge: Cambridge University Press.

McManus, Denis (2013a) "Heidegger on Skepticism, Truth, and Falsehood." In *The Cambridge Companion to Heidegger's* Being and Time, edited by M. Wrathall. Cambridge: Cambridge University Press.

(2013b) "The Provocation to Look and See: Appropriation, Recollection, and Formal Indication." In *Wittgenstein and Heidegger*, edited D. Egan, S. Reynolds, and A. Wendland. New York: Routledge.

McMullin, Irene (2013) *Time and the Shared World*. Evanston: Northwestern University Press.

Merleau-Ponty, Maurice (2013) *Phenomenology of Perception*. Translated by D. Landes. New York: Routledge.

Minar, Edward (2001) "Heidegger's Response to Skepticism in *Being and Time*." In *Future Pasts*, edited by J. Floyd and S. Shieh. Oxford: Oxford University Press.

Moore, G. E. (1959) "Proof of an External World." In *Philosophical Papers*. London: George Allen and Unwin.

Sartre, Jean-Paul (1998) *Being and Nothingness*. Translated by H. Barnes. New York: Routledge.

   (2007) *Existentialism Is a Humanism*. Translated by C. Macomber. New Haven: Yale University Press.

Stroud, Barry (1984) *The Significance of Philosophical Scepticism*. Oxford: Oxford University Press.

Von Hermann, Friedrich-Wilhelm (2013) *Hermeneutics and Reflection*. Toronto: University of Toronto Press.

Westerlund, Frederik (2020) *Heidegger and the Problem of Phenomena*. London: Bloomsbury.

White, Carol (2009) *Time and Death*. New York: Routledge.

Withy, Katherine (2021) "We Are a Conversation." In *Language and Phenomenology*, edited by C. Engelland. New York: Routledge.

   (2022) "Heidegger on Human Being." In *Human*, edited by K. Hübner. Oxford: Oxford University Press.

Withy, Katherine and Askonas, Jon (2019) "Thinking Failure in the War in Iraq." In *Why Philosophy?*, edited by P. D. Bubbio and J. Malpas. Berlin: DeGruyter.

Wrathall, Mark (2021a) "Comportment." In *The Heidegger Lexicon*, edited by M. Wrathall. Cambridge: Cambridge University Press.

   (2021b) "Fourfold." In *The Heidegger Lexicon*, edited by M. Wrathall. Cambridge: Cambridge University Press.

Zahavi, Dan (2003) "How to Investigate Subjectivity: Natorp and Heidegger on Reflection." *Continental Philosophy Review* 36: 155–176.

Acknowledgments

I would like to thank Filippo Casati, Ian Martel, and an anonymous reviewer for their detailed comments, corrections, and suggestions. Portions of this work were presented at annual meetings of the American Society for Existential Phenomenology and the International Society for Phenomenological Studies. The feedback I received on those occasions has been tremendously helpful.

Cambridge Elements

The Philosophy of Martin Heidegger

About the Editors

Filippo Casati
Lehigh University

Filippo Casati is an Assistant Professor at Lehigh University. He has published an array of articles in such venues as The British Journal for the History of Philosophy, Synthese, Logic et Analyse, Philosophia, Philosophy Compass and The European Journal of Philosophy. He is the author of Heidegger and the Contradiction of Being (Routledge) and, with Daniel O. Dahlstrom, he edited Heidegger on logic (Cambridge University Press).

Daniel O. Dahlstrom
Boston University

Daniel O. Dahlstrom, John R. Silber Professor of Philosophy at Boston University, has edited twenty volumes, translated Mendelssohn, Schiller, Hegel, Husserl, Heidegger, and Landmann-Kalischer, and authored Heidegger's Concept of Truth (2001), The Heidegger Dictionary (2013; second extensively expanded edition, 2023), Identity, Authenticity, and Humility (2017) and over 185 essays, principally on 18th–20th century German philosophy. With Filippo Casati, he edited Heidegger on Logic (Cambridge University Press).

About the Series

A continual source of inspiration and controversy, the work of Martin Heidegger challenges thinkers across traditions and has opened up previously unexplored dimensions of Western thinking. The Elements in this series critically examine the continuing impact and promise of a thinker who transformed early twentieth-century phenomenology, spawned existentialism, gave new life to hermeneutics, celebrated the truthfulness of art and poetry, uncovered the hidden meaning of language and being, warned of "forgetting" being, and exposed the ominously deep roots of the essence of modern technology in Western metaphysics. Concise and structured overviews of Heidegger's philosophy offer original and clarifying approaches to the major themes of Heidegger's work, with fresh and provocative perspectives on its significance for contemporary thinking and existence.

Cambridge Elements

The Philosophy of Martin Heidegger

Elements in the Series

Heidegger on Thinking
Lee Braver

Heidegger's Concept of Science
Paul Goldberg

Heidegger on Poetic Thinking
Charles Bambach

Heidegger on Religion
Benjamin D. Crowe

Heidegger and Kierkegaard
George Pattitson

Heidegger on Technology's Danger and Promise in the Age of AI
Iain D. Thomson

Heidegger on Pressure
Richard Polt

Heidegger and the Elements of (Human) Being
S. Montgomery Ewegen

Heidegger on Ethics
Mahon O'Brien

Heidegger and His Platonic Critics
Antoine Pageau-St-Hilaire

Heidegger on Transcendence
Chad Engelland

Heidegger on Being-in-the-World
David R. Cerbone

A full series listing is available at: www.cambridge.org/EPMH

For EU product safety concerns, contact us at Calle de José Abascal, 56–1°, 28003 Madrid, Spain or eugpsr@cambridge.org.

www.ingramcontent.com/pod-product-compliance
Lightning Source LLC
Chambersburg PA
CBHW060053120226
39575CB00016B/342